5 Ingredients
15 MINUTES

HEARST BOOKS
New York

An Imprint of Sterling Publishing
387 Park Avenue South
New York, NY 10016

ISBN 978-1-61837-150-8

Distributed in Canada by Sterling Publishing
c/o Canadian Manda Group, 165 Dufferin Street
Toronto, Ontario, Canada M6K 3H6
Distributed in the United Kingdom by GMC Distribution Services
Castle Place, 166 High Street, Lewes, East Sussex, England BN7 1XU
Distributed in Australia by Capricorn Link (Australia) Pty. Ltd.
P.O. Box 704, Windsor, NSW 2756, Australia

For information about custom editions, special sales, and premium and corporate purchases, please
contact Sterling Special Sales at 800-805-5489 or specialsales@sterlingpublishing.com.

Manufactured in China

2 4 6 8 10 9 7 5 3 1

www.sterlingpublishing.com

5 Ingredients

15 MINUTES

125 Speedy Recipes

Recipes from **Good Housekeeping** **REDBOOK** **Country Living**

HEARST BOOKS

New York

Contents

18

Foreword: Extra Speedy, Extra Easy

Every single recipe in *5 Ingredients/15 Minutes* is guaranteed to help make your dinner prep a snap. To be included here, a recipe has to be either SPEEDY or EASY—and many of the dishes fall into both categories. What exactly do we mean?

To qualify as SPEEDY, a recipe has to be ready in just 15 minutes or less. Note that we aren't counting the time it takes to boil pasta water or preheat the oven or grill. Start that just as soon as you get home; when you're ready to cook, you're good to go. Look for the special symbol (at right), which indicates a SPEEDY recipe.

To qualify as EASY, a recipe must have 5 ingredients or less—excluding pantry staples like salt (table, coarse, kosher), black pepper, red pepper flakes, oil (olive, canola, vegetable), butter, cooking spray, and flour. In addition to containing so few ingredients, these recipes can also be completed in 45 minutes or less, so they're still great for busy weeknights. You can see pictures of the ingredients needed for each EASY recipe with a quick glance (see example below).

The recipes that are both **SPEEDY** and **EASY** can be made in just 45 minutes or less and use no more than 5 ingredients. Supper simply doesn't get any easier or speedier than that!

Introduction: Meals Made Fast!

YOUR MISSION: Supper on the table, STAT. Start with the recipes in this special issue, which were specifically chosen with your crazy-busy life in mind. But if you go one step further and take a look at how you plan your meals, organize your shopping, and stock and arrange your kitchen, you can shave even more minutes off your meal-prep time. Follow the secrets on the pages that follow and set yourself up to make some incredibly quick and delicious dinners.

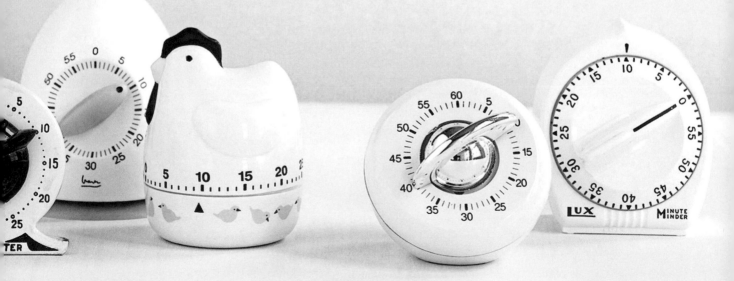

Plan Ahead *and* **Shop Smart!**

- **Set aside time once a week** to create menus for the next 7 days. Read recipes to make sure that you have all the ingredients in the pantry, freezer, or fridge, or on your grocery list.

- **Do a big shopping trip** once a week and eliminate midweek trips to the market. It's more efficient.

- **Arrange your list** by grocery departments and use it as a map to your local market. You'll know exactly where to find everything you need and won't waste any time browsing. Start with the staples aisles first, move on to the perishables, then the refrigerated items. Save the frozen foods for last so they'll stay cold and keep your other perishables cool.

Supermarket **Shortcuts**

Taking advantage of prepared and premade foods can slash the time you spend making dinner. Look for:

- Rotisserie chicken and deli and salad-bar items—they can form the basis of a hearty no-cook dinner. (Check out our recipes on pages 23–29 for terrific meals that begin with a rotisserie chicken.)

- Cleaned, prepared, ready-to-use vegetables, as well as packaged peeled and sliced fresh fruits.

- Bagged salad greens that are cut, washed, and mixed with other veggies—they can go straight from the package to the salad bowl.

- Frozen vegetables. They're not just side dishes: Use them in a stir-fry or toss with noodles or rice.

- Meat, fish, and poultry that's already been seasoned and marinated and is ready for grilling, steaming, stir-frying, and sautéing.

- Precooked and packaged proteins such as chicken pieces, meatballs, and flavored sausages.

4 MORE CLEVER SHOPPING STRATEGIES

1 Stock up at the warehouse store or when there's a sale at your market on your go-to meats, poultry, seafood, or frozen foods. Wrap and freeze these bargain purchases in meal-sized portions.

2 Choose items that naturally cook quickly: Use chicken tenders instead of whole chicken pieces; substitute thinly sliced medallions of pork tenderloin instead of thick bone-in chops; select vegetables cut into matchsticks, which will cook evenly and more quickly than whole or large chunks.

3 Think outside the box—or bottle or package. Buy flavored spice blends to mix into ground beef for meatballs, burgers, or meatloaf with an exotic twist. Bottled creamy salad dressings can top mashed or baked potatoes instead of butter or sour cream. Sauté fresh veggies in a tablespoon of vinaigrette dressing instead of oil. Pick up some garlic-flavored spreadable cheese and thin it with a little milk to make a creamy sauce for pasta.

4 Take advantage of nutritious convenience products: Pre- or partially-baked pizza shells, tortilla wraps, deli meats, sliced cheeses, and prepared salads, such as cole-slaw, broccoli slaw, carrot-and-raisin salad, potato salad, or spinach salad. Be sure to choose the ones with the fewest preservatives and artificial ingredients.

Organize Your **Pantry**

A well-thought-out cupboard frees you up to move fast when it's time to make dinner. Here's how to give yours a makeover:

- **Clear the shelves** and separate foods into groups (baking goods, sauces, etc.).

- **Throw out anything** that's expired and donate multiple products to a needy organization. (You will never use 10 unopened jars of olives.)

- **Put backups** on the top shelf.

- **Place jars and cans** on tiered risers so you can see what you've got.

- **Dump bags of sugar and flour** into airtight clear canisters. They're much less messy than sacks.

- **Place spices on a lazy Susan.** That way, you won't have to claw your way to the back of the shelf to find the cumin!

- **Create sections.** Use colored tape and a Sharpie to label shelves, then stick loose items in bins so the areas don't flow into one another.

- **Store heavy items** on the floor.

- **Ditch bulky boxes** and fill an over-the-door shoe bag with cereal bars, soup packets, and tea bags.

Grocery Checklist **System**

Now that your pantry is in shape, make sure you have these staples on hand. Create a time-to-restock list by hanging a clipboard on the cabinet door.

- Quick-cooking white and brown rice, couscous, and other grains that are fast to make
- Flavored rice mixes
- Pasta in several shapes
- Canned broths and soups, packaged soup mixes
- Canned tomato products: crushed, diced, and sauces
- Canned tuna and salmon
- Canned and dried fruit
- Canned beans
- Nuts
- Peanut butter or other nut butters

- Assorted crackers
- Oils: extra virgin and light olive oils, vegetable, canola, sesame, and a nut oil
- Dried herbs and spices and herb- and-spice blends
- Condiments: vinegars, relishes, pickles, chutneys, mustards, ketchup, olives, sun-dried tomatoes, pesto, salsas
- Salad dressings and bottled sauces (steak, barbecue, soy, peanut, curry, etc.)
- Sweeteners: sugar or sugar substitutes, honey, jams
- Onions, garlic, shallots, ginger, potatoes
- Chocolate chips and baking chocolate

Add Some **Excitement**

Keep these versatile products on hand to give everyday foods extraordinary flavor in no time flat.

- **Bruschetta mix** Stir into pasta for a light sauce, or toss with lettuce and toasted bread cubes for a quick panzanella salad.
- **Garlic paste** Mix a dab into meat when making burgers or meatloaf.
- **Green curry paste** Add to skillet with vegetable oil for a stir-fry that packs a real punch.
- **Sun-dried tomato pesto** Stir into cream cheese for a quick dip, use to marinate poultry, or spread on sandwich bread.
- **Hoisin sauce** Use as a dip for grilled vegetables, a glaze for chicken, or a spread for an Asian-Inspired wrap.
- **Grainy Dijon mustard** Rub on a pork tenderloin before roasting for a tasty crust, or stir into mayo for a tangy sandwich spread.
- **Mango chutney** Use to glaze chicken breasts, or stir into plain nonfat yogurt with chopped fresh cilantro as a condiment for grilled lamb or poultry.
- **Seasoned rice vinegar** Mix with canola oil and soy sauce to make an Asian vinaigrette, or simply toss with salad greens for a fat-free dressing.
- **Worcestershire sauce** Splash it on sautéed mushrooms or sprinkle atop roasted potatoes.

Useful **Utensils**

- **Knives:** You need a paring knife for trimming vegetables and fruits; a chef's knife for fast slicing and chopping; and a serrated knife to cut through delicate foods like bread, tomatoes, and cake.

- **Indoor grill pan** for cooking without oil; it preheats fast and leaves familiar grill marks on food.

- **Microplane grater** for grating hard cheeses, citrus peels, garlic, and ginger.

- **Heavy 12-inch nonstick skillet** with lid, for browning, sautéing, stir-frying, and making sauces.

- **Heat-proof silicone spatulas** in a few sizes.

- **Kitchen scissors** for snipping fresh herbs or cutting homemade pizza into slices.

Quick-Prep Tips

- **Put up water** to boil for rice and pasta as soon as you get home. While the water is coming to a boil, brown the meat or sauté onions.

- **If using ground beef** in a recipe, brown it the previous evening, then let it cool, bag, and refrigerate.

- **Use your microwave** to partially cook ingredients that normally take a long time to make, such as potatoes and other root veggies: Put them in a microwave-safe bowl with a tablespoon of water, cover, and steam.

- **Make enough for 2 meals** and turn leftovers into different dishes later in the week. For example, cook up a pot of chili for dinner Monday night and use the leftovers for tacos or to top baked potatoes on Wednesday.

- **Freeze leftovers** in individual servings, and you'll have a stockpile of quick and healthy meals whenever you need them.

- **Get your kids to help out** by setting the table, pouring milk, and doing other simple tasks.

Time-Saving Appliances

- **Immersion blender** for pureeing soups, and making gravies, dips, and sauces.

- **Microwave oven** for defrosting frozen meats, fish, and poultry; getting a jump-start on slow-cooking foods such as potatoes; reheating leftovers; melting butter, cheese, and chocolate; steaming vegetables.

- **Mini food processor** with changeable cutting disks for chopping, slicing, and shredding.

When dinner needs to be ready ASAP, bird is the word. *Really* in a hurry? Check out our recipes that start with rotisserie chicken.

CHICKEN
ON THE DOUBLE

Orange-Peppercorn Chicken

From Redbook

Total time **15 minutes**

MAKES 4 MAIN-DISH SERVINGS

- 4 **baby bok choy (½ lb. total), halved lengthwise**
- 4 **boneless chicken breast halves (4 oz. each)**
- 1½ **Tbsp. chopped pink peppercorns**
- 1 **orange, zested and juiced**
  Salt
- 2 **Tbsp. julienned fresh ginger**
- 6 **finely chopped green onions**
- 3 **Tbsp. soy sauce**
- 2 **Tbsp. rice vinegar**
- 2 **Tbsp. canola oil**
- 1 **Tbsp. minced peeled fresh ginger**
- 1 **tsp. minced garlic**
  Sugar

1. Line 10-inch Asian bamboo steamer with bok choy. Rub chicken with peppercorns and 1 tablespoon orange zest, then season with ¼ teaspoon salt; place on top of bok choy. Sprinkle with julienned ginger. Place bamboo cover on steamer; steam over large pot of simmering water 8 to 10 minutes or until chicken is no longer pink in the thickest parts when slit with knife.
2. Meanwhile, in small bowl, combine onions, 3 tablespoons orange juice, soy sauce, vinegar, oil, minced ginger, garlic, and pinch of sugar. Serve chicken and bok choy with sauce.

Each serving About 263 calories, 26 g protein, 8 g carbohydrate, 14 g total fat (2 g saturated), 2 g fiber, 65 mg cholesterol, 905 mg sodium.

STEAM HEAT
That's the quick-cook method behind Orange-Peppercorn Chicken.

4 INGREDIENTS

Jamaican Jerk Chicken *with* Sweet Potatoes

From Good Housekeeping

Active time **15 minutes**
Total time **40 minutes**

MAKES 4 MAIN-DISH SERVINGS

- 1½ lb. sweet potatoes, cut into 1-inch chunks
  Salt and pepper
- 4 tsp. olive oil
- 1 bunch green onions (about 6), each cut into 1-inch pieces
- 1 chicken (3½ to 4 lb.), cut into 8 pieces and skin removed from all pieces but wings
- 1 Tbsp. jerk seasoning

1. Preheat oven to 450°F. In large bowl, toss sweet potatoes with ¼ teaspoon salt, ⅛ teaspoon freshly ground black pepper, and 2 teaspoons oil until coated. Arrange potato chunks in 15½" by 10½" jelly-roll pan and roast 20 minutes. Add onions to pan; stir to coat onions with oil, and continue to roast 10 minutes longer or until vegetables are tender and golden.
2. Meanwhile, line another 15½" by 10½" jelly-roll pan with nonstick foil. In large bowl, toss chicken pieces with jerk seasoning, ¼ teaspoon salt, and remaining 2 teaspoons oil until coated. Arrange chicken in pan, and roast 25 minutes or until juices run clear when thickest part of chicken is pierced with tip of knife.
3. Serve chicken with potato mixture.

Each serving About 475 calories, 48 g protein, 31 g carbohydrate, 17 g total fat (4 g saturated), 4 g fiber, 141 mg cholesterol, 655 mg sodium.

Tandoori
Chicken
Skewers

From Redbook

Total time **12 minutes**

MAKES 4 MAIN-DISH SERVINGS

- **1 cup plain yogurt**
- **½ cup diced seedless cucumber**
- **½ cup diced chopped tomato**
- **½ cup diced radishes**
- **2 Tbsp. chopped fresh mint**
- **¾ tsp. ground cumin**
- **Salt**
- **¼ cup bottled or homemade buttermilk or ranch dressing**
- **¼ tsp. chili powder**
- **4 thin-sliced chicken breast cutlets (6 oz. each), each cut into 3 lengthwise strips**
- **Tomato couscous (optional)**

1. Preheat broiler; line broiler pan with nonstick foil.

2. In small bowl, combine ¾ cup yogurt, cucumber, tomato, radishes, mint, ½ teaspoon cumin, and ¼ teaspoon salt; set aside Tomato-Cucumber Sauce.

3. In another small bowl, combine remaining ¼ cup yogurt, dressing, remaining ¼ teaspoon cumin, chili powder, and ¼ teaspoon salt.

4. Thread chicken onto metal skewers. Brush with basting sauce, and broil 4 inches from heat for 2 to 3 minutes. Turn skewers, baste again, and broil 2 to 3 minutes longer. Serve chicken with Tomato-Cucumber Sauce and couscous, if desired.

Each serving without couscous About 292 calories, 37 g protein, 7 g carbohydrate, 12 g total fat (3 g saturated), 1 g fiber, 102 mg cholesterol, 598 mg sodium.

COSTARS
Chicken skewers pair well with grains like couscous (shown here) or basmati rice.

Crispy
Chicken

From Redbook

Total time **15 minutes**

MAKES 4 MAIN-DISH SERVINGS

- **1 large egg**
- **1 tsp. roasted ground cumin**
- **1 cup Italian-seasoned panko (Japanese-style bread crumbs)**
- **4 boneless, skinless chicken-breast halves (5 oz. each)**
- **3 Tbsp. olive oil**

1. In medium bowl, whisk egg and cumin. On sheet of waxed paper, spread bread crumbs. Dip chicken into egg mixture, then coat in bread crumbs.
2. In large nonstick skillet on medium, heat oil. Cook chicken 10 minutes, turning every few minutes until crisp.
3. If desired, serve chicken with salad of tomato, avocado, and red onion drizzled with olive oil and lime juice.

Each serving without salad About 362 calories, 32 g protein, 16 g carbohydrate, 17 g total fat (2 g saturated), 0 g fiber, 125 mg cholesterol, 487 mg sodium.

Chicken Sausage Skewers *with* Cheesy Polenta

From Redbook

Total time **15 minutes**

MAKES 4 MAIN-DISH SERVINGS

- **1 lb. Italian chicken sausage**
- **2 zucchini, cut into ½-inch pieces**
- **1 red onion, cut into 1-inch pieces**
  Olive oil
- **1 cup quick-cooking or instant polenta**
  Kosher salt and pepper
- **4 oz. fontina cheese, diced**
- **¼ cup freshly grated Parmesan cheese**
- **2 Tbsp. butter**

1. Place sausages in medium nonstick skillet; add about ½ inch of water. Cover; cook on medium until sausage firms up, 2 to 3 minutes. Remove from skillet; cut into big chunks.
2. Thread sausage, zucchini, and onion pieces alternately onto 4 (12-inch) skewers. Brush skewers with oil.
3. Preheat outdoor grill or indoor grill pan. Place skewers on hot grill, and cook 10 minutes or until sausage is cooked through, turning frequently and brushing with oil, as needed.
4. Meanwhile, in large saucepan, heat 3 cups water to boiling. Gradually whisk in polenta, ¼ teaspoon salt, and ¼ teaspoon freshly ground black pepper. Cook, whisking frequently, for 2 to 3 minutes or until thick and smooth. Remove from heat. Stir in cheeses and butter. Spoon onto plates; top with skewers.

Each serving About 544 calories, 31 g protein, 38 g carbohydrate, 30 g total fat (14 g saturated), 4 g fiber, 121 mg cholesterol, 1,330 mg sodium.

4 INGREDIENTS

Lemon-Oregano
Chicken

From Redbook

Total time **15 minutes**

MAKES 4 MAIN-DISH SERVINGS

- **4** boneless, skinless chicken-breast halves (5 oz. each)
- **3** Tbsp. fresh lemon juice
- **3** Tbsp. olive oil
- **2** Tbsp. chopped fresh oregano leaves
- **2** tsp. garlic paste
- **½** tsp. crushed red pepper flakes

  Kosher salt

1. In bowl, toss chicken with lemon juice, oil, oregano, garlic paste, red pepper flakes, and ½ teaspoon salt.
2. Preheat outdoor grill or indoor grill pan. Place chicken on hot grill, and cook 6 minutes per side, turning once or twice until cooked through.

Each serving About 254 calories, 29 g protein, 2 g carbohydrate, 14 g total fat (2 g saturated), 0 g fiber, 78 mg cholesterol, 310 mg sodium.

GREEN BEANS with TOMATOES & PINE NUTS

From Redbook

Total time **10 minutes**

MAKES 6 SIDE-DISH SERVINGS

In boiling salted water, cook 1½ pounds trimmed, cut **green beans** 3 to 5 minutes; drain and rinse. In large bowl, toss green beans with 2 **tomatoes,** cut into wedges; 2 tablespoons olive oil; 2 tablespoons chopped fresh **mint;** and 2 tablespoons **pine nuts** (optional). Season to taste with **salt** and freshly ground **black pepper.** Top with **Parmesan** curls.

Each serving About 79 calories, 2 g protein, 9 g carbohydrate, 5 g total fat (1 g saturated), 3 g fiber, 0 mg cholesterol, 57 mg sodium.

QUICK SPUDS

For 4 side-dish servings, microwave 2 cups diced potatoes until soft. Mash with 1½ tablespoons butter and salt and black pepper to taste (65 calories per serving).

Chicken Sausage *with* Warm Chickpea Salad

From Redbook

Total time **10 minutes**

MAKES 4 MAIN-DISH SERVINGS

- **8 fully cooked chicken sausages (1½ lb. total), cut into 1½-inch pieces**
- **4 Tbsp. olive oil**
- **1 Tbsp. garlic paste**
- **2 cans (15 oz. each) chickpeas, rinsed and drained**
- **2 Tbsp. fresh thyme**
  Kosher salt and pepper
- **4 jarred roasted red and yellow bell peppers, diced**
- **1 cup cherry tomatoes, halved**
- **16 pitted kalamata olives**
- **1 lemon, zested and juiced**
- **4 cups arugula**

1. Preheat outdoor grill or indoor grill pan on medium-high. Place sausages on hot grill. Cook sausages 6 to 7 minutes, or until browned and heated through, turning frequently.
2. Meanwhile, in large nonstick skillet on medium-high, heat 2 tablespoons oil. Add garlic paste; cook 30 seconds, stirring . Add chickpeas, thyme, 1 teaspoon salt, and ½ teaspoon freshly ground black pepper, stirring until coated, about 2 minutes. Stir in peppers, tomatoes, and olives; cook until heated through, about 2 minutes.
3. Pour mixture into large bowl. Stir in remaining 2 tablespoons oil, 1 teaspoon lemon zest, and 2 tablespoons lemon juice. Add arugula, tossing gently to combine. Serve salad with sausages.

Each serving About 674 calories, 40 g protein, 42 g carbohydrate, 37 g total fat (6 g saturated), 10 g fiber, 132 mg cholesterol, 2,873 mg sodium.

Sticky Chicken

From Redbook

Total time **12 minutes**

MAKES 4 MAIN-DISH SERVINGS

- ¼ **cup hoisin sauce**
- 3 **Tbsp. canola oil**
- 1 **Tbsp. grated fresh ginger**
- 1 **Tbsp. honey**
- 1 **Tbsp. soy sauce**
- 2½ **tsp. hot red chili sauce (Sriracha)**
- 1½ **tsp. minced garlic**
- 4 **boneless, skinless chicken-breast halves (5 oz. each)**

1. In large bowl, whisk hoisin sauce, 1 tablespoon oil, ginger, honey, soy sauce, chili sauce, and garlic. Add chicken to bowl and toss.

2. In large nonstick skillet on medium, heat remaining 2 tablespoons oil. Add chicken; cook 10 minutes, turning once, until cooked through.

3. If desired, serve with steamed bok choy and rice.

Each serving without sides About 275 calories, 29 g protein, 9 g carbohydrate, 13 g total fat (2 g saturated), 0 g fiber, 79 mg cholesterol, 433 mg sodium.

SHORTCUT SIDES

The only element missing from some of our quick-fix dinners: a fill-you-up starch like pasta, rice, or a whole grain. To add inexpensive, healthy calories to your family's meal, keep a supply of these speedy sides on hand. All are easy to make and low in fat, and can be seasoned with sauce from one of our dinner recipes or with an add-in (see "Add Some Excitement," page 7).

Couscous Available in plain or whole wheat, it's table-ready in **5 minutes.** Season with lemon juice and chopped fresh basil (or any herb from your garden).

Microwavable rice
Ready in under **2 minutes.** Try jasmine, basmati, or brown varieties; stir in fresh spinach or thawed frozen peas to boost vitamins and minerals.

Quinoa This grain is higher in protein and lower in carbs than most. Toast in skillet; cook in stock or water for **12 minutes.** Sprinkle with soy sauce, sesame oil, or lemon juice.

 +  + + 🥕 + 🫛

Roasted Tarragon Chicken *with* Carrots & Peas

From Redbook

Active time **10 minutes**
Total time **40 minutes**

MAKES 4 MAIN-DISH SERVINGS

- 3 **Tbsp. unsalted butter, softened**
- 1 **Tbsp. chopped fresh tarragon leaves**
  Kosher salt and pepper
- 1 **chicken (3¼ lb.), quartered and wing tips removed, trimmed of excess fat**
- 1 **Tbsp. olive oil**
- ½ **cup reduced-sodium chicken broth**
- 2-3 **bunches baby carrots (about 16 carrots total), tops trimmed to 1 inch**
- 2 **cups frozen (thawed) or fresh green peas**

1. Preheat oven to 400°F. In small cup, combine butter, tarragon, ¼ teaspoon salt, and ¼ teaspoon freshly ground black pepper. Smear herb-butter mixture under skin of chicken pieces (and smear skin with any remaining herb butter).

2. In large cast-iron or ovenproof nonstick skillet on medium-high, heat oil. Add chicken, skin side down; cook 6 minutes or until golden brown. Turn pieces; lightly brown second side 2 minutes. Add broth to skillet and place in oven. Roast 30 minutes, until chicken is cooked through.

3. Meanwhile, bring 4 cups water to boiling in medium saucepan; add carrots and blanch 3 minutes, until very crisp-tender. Drain; refresh under cold water.

4. Remove chicken to serving plate; keep warm. Place skillet with drippings on stovetop on medium heat. Stir in carrots and peas; cook, stirring constantly, 2 to 3 minutes, until vegetables are crisp-tender. Spoon onto plates and top with chicken.

Each serving About 665 calories, 43 g protein, 14 g carbohydrate, 48 g total fat (16 g saturated), 5 g fiber, 187 mg cholesterol, 366 mg sodium.

5 INGREDIENTS

CRAVING CRUNCH?
Serve the potato salad on a bed of torn Boston or green leaf lettuce.

Creamy Dijon
Drumsticks

From Good Housekeeping

Active time **20 minutes**
Total time **45 minutes**

MAKES 4 MAIN-DISH SERVINGS

- 1½ **lb. small red potatoes, each cut in half (or quarters if larger)**
- **Salt and pepper**
- 8 **medium chicken drumsticks (2¼ lb.), skin removed**
- 3 **Tbsp. plus ¼ cup Dijonnaise (creamy mustard)**
- ⅔ **cup panko (Japanese-style bread crumbs)**
- 2 **medium celery stalks, thinly sliced**

1. Preheat oven to 450°F. In 4-quart saucepan, place potatoes, enough water to cover, and ½ teaspoon salt; heat to boiling on high. Reduce heat to medium-low; cover saucepan and simmer potatoes 10 to 12 minutes or until just fork-tender.

2. Meanwhile, line 15½" by 10½" jelly-roll pan with nonstick foil. Brush chicken with 3 tablespoons Dijonnaise and coat with panko, pressing to adhere. Place chicken on prepared pan and bake 25 minutes or until crumbs are golden and juices run clear when thickest part of chicken is pierced with tip of knife.

3. Drain potatoes well and place in medium bowl. Add celery, ½ teaspoon freshly ground black pepper, and remaining ¼ cup Dijonnaise; stir to coat vegetables.

4. To serve, arrange salad and chicken on dinner plates.

Each serving About 405 calories, 34 g protein, 47 g carbohydrate, 11 g total fat (1 g saturated), 4 g fiber, 110 mg cholesterol, 540 mg sodium.

5 INGREDIENTS

Maple-Roasted Chicken Thighs *with* Sweet Potatoes

From Good Housekeeping

Active time **5 minutes**
Total time **45 minutes**

MAKES 4 MAIN-DISH SERVINGS

- **4** large skinless chicken thighs (about 1½ lb. with bones)
- **2** small sweet potatoes (about 1 lb. total), peeled and cut into 1-inch chunks
- **1** small onion, cut into 1-inch pieces
- **8** oz. baby carrots, cut into 1-inch chunks
- **¼** cup maple syrup
- Salt and pepper

1. Preheat oven to 450°F.
2. In 15½" by 10½" jelly-roll pan or large shallow roasting pan, combine chicken, sweet potato chunks, onion, carrots, syrup, 1 teaspoon salt, and ½ teaspoon freshly ground black pepper; toss to coat.
3. Roast mixture 40 to 45 minutes or until juices run clear when thickest part of thigh is pierced with tip of knife and liquid in pan thickens slightly, stirring vegetables once and turning chicken over halfway through roasting.

Each serving About 290 calories, 21 g protein, 41 g carbohydrate, 4 g total fat (1 g saturated), 4 g fiber, 80 mg cholesterol, 695 mg sodium.

5 INGREDIENTS

CRISPY ROSEMARY POTATO CAKES

From Country Living

Active time **15 minutes**
Total time **30 minutes**

MAKES 6 SIDE-DISH SERVINGS

In medium skillet on medium-low, heat 1 tablespoon **olive oil.** Add 1½ cups chopped **onion,** 1 tablespoon finely chopped **rosemary,** ½ teaspoon **salt,** and ½ teaspoon freshly ground **black pepper;** cook until onion is soft and golden, about 7 minutes. Transfer to large bowl; add 3 cups leftover **mashed potatoes** or 1 package refrigerated premade mashed potatoes (such as Simply Potatoes) and mix. Season with salt and pepper. Spread 1 cup **panko** (Japanese-style bread crumbs) in shallow dish. In large skillet on medium-high, heat 1 tablespoon **olive oil.** Using ⅓ cup measure, form potato mixture into 12 cakes. Gently press panko on both sides of each cake. Cook cakes in batches (adding more olive oil as needed), turning once, until golden brown and heated through, about 8 minutes.

Each serving About 230 calories, 2 g protein, 28 g carbohydrate, 12 g total fat (1 g saturated), 2 g fiber, 12 mg cholesterol, 548 mg sodium.

**Start with a store-bought
ROTISSERIE CHICKEN
and follow these simple, delicious
recipes to put
a meal on the table *now***

Asian Chicken & Mango Salad

From Redbook

Total time **15 minutes**

MAKES 4 MAIN-DISH SERVINGS

1½ **Tbsp. grated peeled fresh
ginger root**

1½ **tsp. minced garlic**

⅔ **cup canola oil**

⅓ **cup rice vinegar**

1½ **Tbsp. toasted sesame oil**

¼ **cup reduced-sodium soy sauce**

2 **Tbsp. honey**

Salt and pepper

1 **small cooked rotisserie chicken,
skin and bones removed, and
meat shredded**

1 **large ripe mango, halved,
pitted, and diced**

1 **large seedless cucumber,
quartered lengthwise and
cut into chunks**

1 **small red onion, thinly sliced**

3 **large bunches watercress,
separated into sprigs, or 8 cups
mixed salad greens**

Lime wedges, for garnish

1. In 2-cup jar, combine ginger, garlic, canola oil, vinegar, sesame oil, soy sauce, ¼ cup water, honey, and ½ teaspoon freshly ground black pepper. Cover jar with tight-fitting lid and shake well to dissolve honey. Store dressing covered in refrigerator up to 3 weeks. (Makes about 1½ cups.)
2. In large bowl, toss chicken with mango, cucumber, onion, and ½ teaspoon salt. Add ½ cup dressing and toss to lightly coat. Serve chicken salad over watercress or mixed greens. Garnish with lime wedges.

Each serving About 438 calories, 37 g protein, 26 g carbohydrate, 23 g total fat (4 g saturated), 3 g fiber, 118 mg cholesterol, 1,121 mg sodium.

Fiesta Tex-Mex Salad

From Good Housekeeping

Total time **15 minutes**

MAKES 4 MAIN-DISH SERVINGS

- **1** large head red leaf lettuce, chopped
- **2** cups fresh corn kernels
- **1** can (15 oz.) black beans, rinsed and drained
- **4** radishes, thinly sliced
- **½** cup shredded Monterey Jack cheese
- **6** Tbsp. bottled or homemade cilantro-lime dressing
- **1** large cooked rotisserie chicken, skin and bones removed, and meat cubed
- **1** avocado, cut into ¼-inch chunks
- **½** cup coarsely crushed tortilla chips

In large bowl, toss lettuce, corn, beans, radishes, and cheese with dressing. Top salad with chicken, avocado, and tortilla chips.

Each serving About 741 calories, 56 g protein, 44 g carbohydrate, 39 g total fat (8 g saturated), 13 g fiber, 139 mg cholesterol, 1,118 mg sodium.

Dijon **Chicken Salad** *with* Bacon

From Good Housekeeping

Total time **15 minutes**

MAKES 4 MAIN-DISH SERVINGS

- **4** slices bacon, each cut in half
- **2** Tbsp. apple cider vinegar
- **1** Tbsp. Dijon mustard
- **1** Tbsp. olive oil

  Salt and pepper
- **1** bag (9 oz.) cut hearts of romaine
- **2** cups shredded skinless rotisserie chicken meat (about 10 oz.)

1. In 2-quart saucepan on medium, cook bacon 5 to 6 minutes or until browned. With tongs or slotted spoon, transfer bacon to paper towels to drain. Discard all but 1 tablespoon bacon drippings from saucepan.

2. With whisk, add vinegar, mustard, oil, ¼ teaspoon salt, and ¼ teaspoon coarsely ground black pepper to drippings in saucepan; heat to boiling on medium. Remove from heat.

3. Place romaine in large serving bowl. Pour hot dressing over romaine; toss until coated. Add chicken, and toss until well mixed. Crumble bacon; sprinkle over salad.

Each serving About 240 calories, 24 g protein, 1 g carbohydrate, 15 g total fat (4 g saturated), 6 g fiber, 72 mg cholesterol, 405 mg sodium.

5 INGREDIENTS

5 INGREDIENTS

Pulled-Chicken Sandwiches

From Good Housekeeping

Total time **10 minutes**

MAKES 6 SANDWICHES

- 1 **small cooked rotisserie chicken, skin and bones removed, and meat shredded**
- 1 **cup bottled or homemade barbecue sauce**
- ¼ **cup red wine vinegar**
- 6 **kaiser rolls, split**
- ½ **lb. deli coleslaw**
  Carrot and celery sticks (optional)

1. In 2-quart saucepan on medium, combine chicken, barbecue sauce, ½ cup water, and vinegar. Cook sauce 5 minutes or until hot, stirring.

2. Spoon chicken mixture onto bottom halves of rolls and top with coleslaw and top of roll. Serve with carrot and celery sticks, if desired.

Each sandwich About 436 calories, 28 g protein, 51 g carbohydrate, 12 g total fat (3 g saturated), 2 g fiber, 70 mg cholesterol, 1,011 mg sodium.

Pear & Chicken Heros

From Country Living

Total time **10 minutes**

MAKES 4 SANDWICHES

- **2 Tbsp.** chopped fresh parsley
- **5 Tbsp.** bottled or homemade balsamic vinaigrette
- **1** plain or whole wheat baguette, about 18 inches long, split lengthwise
- **1** small cooked rotisserie chicken, breast meat sliced (reserve remaining chicken for another use)
- Salt and pepper
- **1** Bartlett pear, thinly sliced

1. In small bowl, stir together parsley and vinaigrette. Drizzle both sides of bread with half of vinaigrette.

2. Layer chicken on bottom half of baguette and season with salt and freshly ground black pepper. Drizzle with half of remaining vinaigrette. Layer pear slices over chicken. Drizzle with remaining vinaigrette and top with remaining half of baguette. Cut baguette into 4 sandwiches.

Each sandwich About 411 calories, 33 g protein, 52 g carbohydrate, 9 g total fat (2 g saturated), 7 g fiber, 76 mg cholesterol, 502 mg sodium.

5 INGREDIENTS

Tex-Mex Chicken **Wraps**

From Redbook

Total time **15 minutes**

MAKES 4 WRAPS

- 2 Tbsp. olive oil
- 5 Tbsp. fresh lime juice
- 1 tsp. ground chili powder
- 1 large cooked rotisserie chicken, skin and bones removed, and meat shredded
- 1 can (15.5 oz.) black beans, rinsed and drained
- 2 cups cherry tomatoes, halved
- 1 cup corn kernels
- ⅓ cup diced red onion
- 2 Tbsp. diced jalapeño pepper
- 1 ripe Hass avocado, peeled and pitted
  Salt
- 4 chili or whole wheat flour tortillas (10- to 12-inch)
- 2 cups shredded iceberg lettuce
- 1½ cups shredded Cheddar or Monterey Jack cheese

1. In large bowl, whisk together oil, 4 tablespoons lime juice, and chili powder. Add chicken, beans, tomatoes, corn, onion, and jalapeño; toss.

2. In small bowl, mash avocado, remaining 1 tablespoon lime juice, and ¼ teaspoon salt.

3. Lay tortillas on work surface. Divide chicken mixture among tortillas, placing in a strip along bottom, 1 inch from edges. Top each tortilla with avocado mixture, lettuce, and cheese, dividing evenly. Fold each tortilla and roll up.

Each wrap About 909 calories, 65 g protein, 67 g carbohydrate, 43 g total fat (15 g saturated), 14 g fiber, 171 mg cholesterol, 1,685 mg sodium.

Herbed Chicken & Hot Pepper **Sandwiches**

From Country Living

Total time **10 minutes**

MAKES 8 SANDWICHES

- ½ **cup mayonnaise**
- 1 **tsp. finely chopped fresh rosemary**
- 4 **baguettes (each 10 inches long), split horizontally**
- 3 **oz. hot capocollo or salami, thinly sliced**
- 1 **cup pickled hot peppers, thinly sliced**
- 1 **small rotisserie chicken, skin and bones removed, and meat thinly sliced**
- 6 **oz. fontina cheese, sliced ¼-inch thick**

In small bowl, combine mayonnaise and rosemary. Spread rosemary-mayonnaise on both sides of baguettes. Layer capocollo, peppers, chicken, and fontina on bottom halves of baguettes. Replace tops of bread; cut each sandwich in half, and serve.

Each sandwich About 628 calories, 37 g protein, 64 g carbohydrate, 24 g total fat (8 g saturated), 3 g fiber, 90 mg cholesterol, 2,010 mg sodium.

To keep your family running on schedule (but not running on empty), try one of these hearty weeknight entrées

MEAT
IN MINUTES

Gaucho Steak *with* Grilled Peppers

From Redbook

Total time **15 minutes**

MAKES 4 MAIN-DISH SERVINGS

1½ **lb. skirt steak**

   Coffee spice rub (or your favorite dry rub for steaks)

16 **baby bell peppers**

   Olive oil

8 **warm corn tortillas**

½ **cup crumbled queso fresco**

2 **Tbsp. chopped fresh cilantro**

1. Cut steak into 4 even pieces; coat both sides with rub. Onto 2 skewers, thread bell peppers. Brush steaks and peppers with oil. Preheat outdoor grill or indoor grill pan. Cook peppers 8 to 10 minutes, and cook steaks 3 to 4 minutes per side (for medium rare). Let meat rest 5 minutes; then slice.
2. Serve sliced steak with peppers, tortillas, queso fresco, and cilantro.

Each serving About 536 calories, 41 g protein, 31 g carbohydrate, 26 g total fat (9 g saturated), 5 g fiber, 87 mg cholesterol, 493 mg sodium.

SURPRISING TOUCH

A quick coffee rub gives steak a taste that's rich and savory.

+ + + +

Beef Tenderloin
with Horseradish Mash
& Artichokes

5 INGREDIENTS

From Redbook

Active time **15 minutes**
Total time **35 minutes**

MAKES 4 MAIN-DISH SERVINGS

- **1 lb. baby artichokes (about 8)**
- **1½ lb. baby red new potatoes, quartered**
- **4 Tbsp. olive oil**
- **2 Tbsp. prepared horseradish**
- **Kosher salt**
- **4 beef tenderloin steaks, 1¼-inch thick (6 oz. each)**
- **2 tsp. medium ground mixed peppercorns (red, green, black, and white)**

1. Place steaming basket in large saucepan with tight-fitting lid; fill with 1 inch of water and bring to boiling. Remove tough outer leaves from artichokes and cut ½ inch off the tops. Trim stem ends and lightly peel. Place artichokes, stem end up, in steaming basket. Cover; steam until tender, about 15 minutes. Remove artichokes with tongs to cutting board. Cool, then quarter artichokes lengthwise.
2. Meanwhile, in medium saucepan, bring potatoes and enough water to cover by 1 inch to boiling; cook 15 minutes or until fork tender. Drain well, reserving ½ cup cooking water; return potatoes to saucepan with reserved cooking water, 2 tablespoons oil, horseradish, and ½ teaspoon salt; mash until nearly smooth. Keep warm.
3. Sprinkle steak with peppercorns, gently pressing pepper into meat; season with ½ teaspoon salt. In large nonstick skillet on medium-high, heat 1 tablespoon oil until shimmering; sear steaks 3 minutes or until browned. Continue to cook steaks, turning 6 to 7 minutes or until internal temperature registers 135°F for medium rare. Remove steaks; let rest 5 minutes.
4. Wipe skillet with paper towels and heat remaining 1 tablespoon oil. Add artichokes, and cook 2 minutes or until lightly browned. Serve steaks with mash and artichokes.

Each serving About 514 calories, 38 g protein, 37 g carbohydrate, 23 g total fat (6 g saturated), 6 g fiber, 92 mg cholesterol, 618 mg sodium.

SPEEDY & SPICY
This ground beef dinner is as easy to make as burgers but packs way more flavor.

Beef & Black Bean Chili

From Redbook

Total time **15 minutes**

MAKES 4 MAIN-DISH SERVINGS

- **2 Tbsp. canola oil**
- **1 cup chopped onion**
- **2 tsp. garlic paste**
- **1 lb. ground beef**
- **1 can (14.5 oz.) fire-roasted diced tomatoes, undrained**
- **1 can (15.5 oz.) black beans, rinsed and drained**
- **2 chipotle chiles in adobo sauce, chopped**
- **1 tsp. ground cumin**
- **Kosher salt and pepper**

1. In large saucepan on medium-high, heat oil. Add onion and garlic paste; cook, stirring often until softened, about 2 minutes. Add ground beef, breaking it up and cooking until no longer pink, about 2 minutes.
2. Add tomatoes, black beans, chiles, cumin, salt, and freshly ground black pepper to taste. Bring to boiling, then reduce heat and simmer 10 minutes.
3. Serve chili with desired toppings, including onion, avocado, shredded Cheddar cheese, and sour cream.

Each serving without toppings About 415 calories, 31 g protein, 28 g carbohydrate, 19 g total fat (5 g saturated), 9 g fiber, 74 mg cholesterol, 577 mg sodium.

15 MINUTES

Orange Beef & Asparagus Stir-fry

NO WOK REQUIRED!
A large, nonstick skillet works just fine.

From Redbook

Total time **15 minutes**

MAKES 4 MAIN-DISH SERVINGS

- ¾ cup orange juice
- 3 Tbsp. reduced-sodium soy sauce
- ¼ cup honey
- 1 Tbsp. cornstarch
- 1 tsp. chili oil or ½ tsp. crushed red pepper flakes
- 1 lb. flank steak, cut across the grain into thin strips
- 2 Tbsp. peanut oil or canola oil
- 2 cups asparagus, cut into 1½-inch pieces
- 1 red bell pepper, cut into strips
- ½ cup sliced green onions
- 1 cup shredded carrots
- 2 tsp. grated fresh ginger
- 1 tsp. minced garlic
- ½ cup honey-roasted peanuts

1. In bowl, combine orange juice, soy sauce, honey, cornstarch, and chili oil. Add steak strips, tossing to combine.
2. In large nonstick skillet on high, heat 1 tablespoon oil. Add asparagus and stir-fry 4 minutes. Add bell pepper, onions, and carrots; stir-fry 1 minute. Add ginger and garlic; stir-fry 1 minute. Remove vegetables to bowl.
3. Heat remaining 1 tablespoon oil. Add steak; stir-fry 3 to 4 minutes. Add reserved vegetables and peanuts; stir-fry until heated through. Serve with rice, if desired.

Each serving without rice About 496 calories, 32 g protein, 38 g carbohydrate, 25 g total fat (6 g saturated), 5 g fiber, 74 mg cholesterol, 827 mg sodium.

Quick
Mu Shu Pork

From Good Housekeeping

Total time **15 minutes**

MAKES 4 MAIN-DISH SERVINGS

- 1 **lb. ground pork**
- 1 **Tbsp. dry sherry**
- 2 **Tbsp. lower-sodium soy sauce**
  Pepper
- 1 **Tbsp. vegetable oil**
- 2 **garlic cloves, crushed**
- ¼ **tsp. crushed red pepper flakes**
- 1 **cups diced jicama**
- 1 **bag (14 oz.) coleslaw mix**
- 3 **green onions, thinly sliced,**
  plus additional for garnish
- 1 **tsp. sugar**
- 8 **flour tortillas (8-inch)**
- 8 **tsp. hoisin sauce**

1. In bowl, combine ground pork, sherry, 1 tablespoon soy sauce, and ⅛ teaspoon freshly ground black pepper.

2. In 12-inch skillet on medium-high, heat oil until hot. Add pork mixture in single layer and cook 1 minute without stirring. Cook 1 minute longer or until pork just loses its pink color, stirring. Transfer pork to large bowl.

3. To same skillet, add garlic and red pepper flakes, and cook 10 seconds. Add jicama, coleslaw, and 2 tablespoons water. Cook vegetables 3 minutes or until just tender, stirring.

4. Add onions, sugar, cooked pork, and remaining 1 tablespoon soy sauce; cook 1 minute longer, stirring.

5. Wrap tortillas in damp paper towels and microwave on High 1 minute or until tortillas are warm and pliable.

6. To serve, spread 1 teaspoon hoisin on each tortilla, divide mixture among tortillas, and fold to eat out of hand.

Each serving About 570 calories, 26 g protein, 42 g carbohydrate, 32 g total fat (10 g saturated), 6 g fiber, 82 mg cholesterol, 940 mg sodium.

15 MINUTES

Pork Chops *with* Cider Sauce

From Redbook

Total time **15 minutes**

MAKES 4 MAIN-DISH SERVINGS

- **2** Tbsp. olive oil
- **4** boneless pork chops, ¾- to 1-inch thick (6 oz. each)
- **¼** cup minced onion or shallot
- **1** garlic clove, minced
- **1** cup apple cider
- **2** tsp. cider vinegar
- **1** tsp. Dijon mustard
  Coarse salt and pepper

1. In large heavy skillet on medium-high, heat oil. Add pork chops, and cook 4 to 5 minutes per side, turning once, until cooked through. Place on serving platter; keep warm.

2. Add onions and garlic to skillet; cook, stirring constantly, 1 minute. Add cider, increase heat, and cook 4 minutes, scraping up browned bits on bottom of skillet, until cider is reduced and slightly thickened.

3. Add vinegar, mustard, salt, and freshly ground black pepper to skillet, stirring to combine. Pour over pork. If desired, serve with broccolini and sautéed apple slices.

Each serving without sides About 360 calories, 37 g protein, 9 g carbohydrate, 19 g total fat (5 g saturated), 0 g fiber, 114 mg cholesterol, 119 mg sodium.

15 MINUTES

DINNER EXPRESS
Boneless pork chops cook up ASAP.

 +  +

Maple-Mustard
Glazed
Pork Chops

From Redbook

Active time **6 minutes**
Total time **22 minutes**

MAKES 4 MAIN-DISH SERVINGS

    Oil

  2 **Tbsp. maple syrup**

1½ **Tbsp. whole-grain mustard**

1½ **Tbsp. Dijon mustard**

  1 **tsp. garlic paste**

  4 **boneless pork chops,
     ¾- to 1-inch thick (6 oz. each)**

    Coarse salt and pepper

1. Rub broiler pan with oil to coat. Preheat pan 6 inches from heat source.
2. In small bowl, stir together maple syrup, mustards, and garlic paste to make glaze.
3. Sprinkle pork chops with salt and freshly ground black pepper. Place pork on hot broiler pan and broil 8 or 9 minutes per side, turning once.
4. Spread maple-mustard mixture on top of pork and continue to broil until glaze is bubbly, about 2 minutes. Remove from broiler and serve. If desired, serve with mashed sweet potatoes and green beans.

Each serving without sides About 285 calories, 30 g protein, 9 g carbohydrate, 13 g total fat (4 g saturated), 0 g fiber, 98 mg cholesterol, 316 mg sodium.

**BETTER
THAN EVER**

Pork has always paired
beautifully with fruit.
In this recipe, nectarines
update the concept.

Pork Tenderloin *with* Nectarines

From Good Housekeeping

Active time **15 minutes**
Total time **35 minutes**

MAKES 4 MAIN-DISH SERVINGS

- **4** ripe but firm nectarines, each cut into 4 wedges
- **1** tsp. plus 2 Tbsp. olive oil
  Salt and pepper
- **1¼** lb. pork tenderloin
- **2** Tbsp. white balsamic vinegar
- **1** bunch (6 oz.) watercress, rinsed and tough stems trimmed and discarded

1. Preheat outdoor grill or indoor grill pan. Brush nectarine wedges with 1 teaspoon oil and sprinkle with ⅛ teaspoon salt and ⅛ teaspoon freshly ground black pepper. Place nectarine wedges on hot grill and cook about 10 minutes or until charred and tender, turning once. Transfer nectarines to plate and cover loosely with foil to keep warm.

2. Meanwhile, cut pork tenderloin crosswise into 8 equal pieces. With palm of hand, firmly press on each piece to flatten to about 1-inch-thick medallion. Sprinkle pork evenly with ¼ teaspoon salt and ⅛ teaspoon pepper to season both sides.

3. To same grill, add pork and cook about 10 to 12 minutes or until browned on the outside and still slightly pink in the center, turning once.

4. Meanwhile, make dressing: In small bowl, whisk vinegar, ⅛ teaspoon salt, ⅛ teaspoon pepper, and remaining 2 tablespoons oil until blended. Makes ¼ cup. Remove 1 tablespoon dressing; set aside.

5. In large bowl, toss watercress and remaining dressing. Place on plates and top with pork and nectarines. Drizzle pork with reserved dressing.

Each serving About 325 calories, 32 g protein, 18 g carbohydrate, 14 g total fat (3 g saturated), 3 g fiber, 89 mg cholesterol, 380 mg sodium.

4 INGREDIENTS

Beer-Braised
Pork Chops

From Country Living

Active time **25 minutes**
Total time **35 minutes**

MAKES 4 MAIN-DISH SERVINGS

- 2 **tsp. olive oil**
- 4 **center-cut bone-in pork loin chops (8 oz. each)**

  Salt and pepper
- 2 **Anjou pears, peeled, cored, and cut into wedges (about ¾-inch thick)**
- 1 **bottle (12 oz.) lager beer**
- ¾ **tsp. dried sage or ¾ Tbsp. chopped fresh sage leaves**

1. In large skillet on medium-high, heat oil. Season pork chops with salt and freshly ground black pepper. Add to skillet and sear until lightly browned, about 4 minutes per side. Transfer pork to plate. Drain all but 1 tablespoon fat from pan.
2. Add pears to skillet, and cook until golden, about 6 minutes. Transfer pears to plate with pork. Add beer and sage to pan.
3. With wooden spoon, scrape up caramelized bits from bottom. Return pork and pears to pan; bring to simmer. Partially cover skillet with lid, reduce heat to low, and braise until chops are cooked through, 5 to 7 minutes.
4. Remove pork and pears from pan. Skim away any fat from liquid, increase heat to medium, and cook until sauce is reduced by half, about 10 minutes. Serve chops with pears and sauce.

Each serving About 348 calories, 25 g protein, 15 g carbohydrate, 20 g total fat (4 g saturated), 2 g fiber, 66 mg cholesterol, 483 mg sodium.

Pork Chops & Pears

From Redbook
Total time **15 minutes**

MAKES 4 MAIN-DISH SERVINGS

- ¼ **cup flour**
- **Salt and pepper**
- 4 **boneless loin pork chops, ¾-inch thick (3 to 4 oz. each)**
- 1 **Tbsp. olive oil**
- 1 **Tbsp. unsalted butter**
- ½ **cup white wine or chicken broth**
- ⅓ **cup chopped green onions**
- ¼ **cup heavy cream**
- 1 **tsp. fresh lemon juice**
- 1 **firm ripe pear, cored and cut into slices (about ¾-inch thick)**
- 2 **tsp. chopped fresh flat-leaf parsley**

1. In shallow plate, combine flour with ¼ teaspoon salt and ¼ teaspoon freshly ground black pepper. Add pork chops, tossing to coat.
2. In large skillet on medium-high, heat oil and butter. Add pork and cook, turning once, about 8 minutes total or until cooked through. Remove to plate; tent with foil to keep warm.
3. To same skillet, add wine, onions, cream, lemon juice, ¼ teaspoon salt, and ¼ teaspoon pepper, stirring to scrape up any browned bits and until sauce is thickened, about 5 minutes.
4. Gently stir in pear slices; cook until just heated through, 45 seconds. Pour over pork; sprinkle with parsley.

Each serving About 324 calories, 22 g protein, 14 g carbohydrate, 21 g total fat (9 g saturated), 2 g fiber, 97 mg cholesterol, 356 mg sodium.

ARUGULA & OLIVE SALAD

From Good Housekeeping
Total time **10 minutes**

MAKES 4 SIDE-DISH SERVINGS
Total time **10 minutes**

In large bowl, combine 6 ounces **baby arugula;** 2 **roasted red peppers,**

thinly sliced; ¼ cup pitted **kalamata olives,** halved; 3 tablespoons bottled or homemade **balsamic vinaigrette.** Toss to coat. Divide among serving plates. With vegetable peeler, shave 1 ounce **Parmesan cheese** into paper-thin slices over salads.

Each serving About 125 calories, 4 g protein, 5 g carbohydrate, 10 g total fat (2 g saturated), 1 g fiber, 6 mg cholesterol, 380 mg sodium.

5 INGREDIENTS

Pork Piccata with Grape Tomatoes

From Redbook

Total time **25 minutes**

MAKES 4 MAIN-DISH SERVINGS

- 1 **lemon**
- ¼ **cup dried seasoned bread crumbs**
- 4 **boneless center-cut pork chops, ¾-inch thick (4 oz. each), trimmed**
- 2 **Tbsp. olive oil**
- 2 **Tbsp. unsalted butter**
- 2 **Tbsp. drained capers, rinsed**
- 1 **pint red and/or yellow grape tomatoes**
- **Chopped fresh flat-leaf parsley, for garnish (optional)**

1. Zest lemon with microplane grater and reserve; cut away remaining peel and white pith from lemon and cut into thin slices; seed and halve slices. Spread bread crumbs on waxed paper; coat pork chops with bread crumbs, pressing crumbs firmly into pork.
2. In large nonstick skillet on medium-high, heat 1 tablespoon oil and 1 tablespoon butter. Add pork; cook 3 minutes per side, or until golden on outside and barely pink in thickest part. Transfer to platter. To drippings in skillet, add ⅔ cup water and capers. and boil 1 minute, until liquid is reduced by half; add lemon slices. Remove skillet from heat. Swirl in remaining 1 tablespoon butter until sauce is emulsified; spoon mixture over chops. Cover and keep warm.
3. In medium skillet on high, heat remaining 1 tablespoon oil; add tomatoes. Cook 2 minutes, tossing frequently, until skins start to split and tomatoes soften. Add to platter, and sprinkle with parsley, if you like. Serve pork with orzo or rice, if desired.

Each serving without orzo or rice About 397 calories, 24 g protein, 10 g carbohydrate, 29 g total fat (10 g saturated), 2 g fiber, 83 mg cholesterol, 312 mg sodium.

(ALMOST) READY TO EAT

The editors at *Good Housekeeping* love these extra-convenient, extra-fast accompaniments

Simply Potatoes Refrigerated Mashed Potatoes
Made from fresh spuds, and real butter, whole milk, and half-and-half.

Uncle Ben's Ready Rice Whole Grain Brown
Cooks in just 90 seconds!

Mrs. T's Mini Pierogies
Available in a variety of flavors.

Mann's Fresh-Cut Sweet Potatoes
Saves peeling and cubing.

Mann's Stringless Sugar Snap Peas
Eat them right out of the bag.

Sautéed **Pork Chops** with Kale

From Country Living

Total time **40 minutes**

MAKES 4 MAIN-DISH SERVINGS

- **2 large bunches kale**
- **3 Tbsp. olive oil**
- **Salt and pepper**
- **4 center-cut bone-in pork loin chops (8 oz. each)**
- **3 garlic cloves, finely chopped**
- **Juice of 1 lemon**

1. Cut stems and spines from kale leaves, then roughly chop; wash well (do not dry) and set aside.

2. In large skillet on medium-high, heat 2 tablespoons oil. Season pork chops with salt and freshly ground black pepper. Cook pork about 4 minutes per side until cooked through. Transfer to plate; tent with foil to keep warm.

3. Add remaining 1 tablespoon oil to same skillet. Cook garlic until golden, about 1 minute. Add kale, and cook until tender, about 10 minutes. Sprinkle with lemon juice.

Each serving About 326 calories, 27 g protein, 9 g carbohydrate, 21 g total fat (6 g saturated), 3 g fiber, 81 mg cholesterol, 106 mg sodium.

4 INGREDIENTS

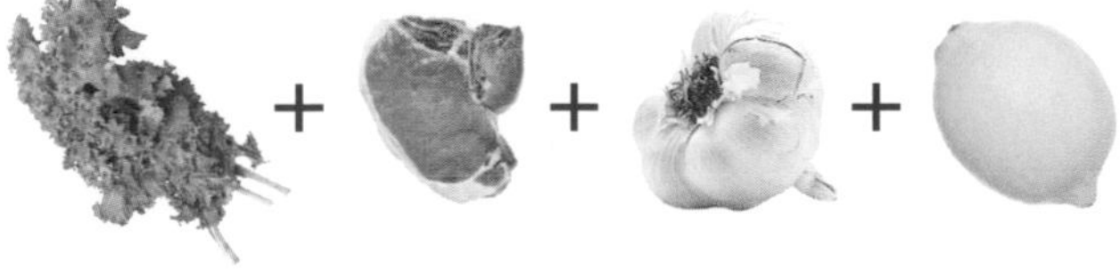

BRUSSELS SPROUTS WITH PANCETTA

From Country Living

Active time **15 minutes**

Total time **30 minutes**

MAKES 4 SIDE-DISH SERVINGS

In medium pan on medium, add 2 tablespoons **olive oil** and 2 ounces **pancetta,** diced; cook until lightly browned, about 3 minutes. Using slotted spoon, transfer pancetta to plate; reserve. Add 1 lb. **Brussels sprouts,** trimmed and quartered; stir for 30 seconds. Add 1 cup water, cover, and reduce heat to medium-low. Steam for 5 minutes. Remove lid, increase heat to medium-high, and cook, stirring occasionally, until sprouts are golden brown, about 15 minutes. Remove from heat and toss in pancetta; 2 ounces **pine nuts,** toasted; and 3 ounces **Romano cheese,** grated. Season with **salt** and freshly ground **black pepper;** serve immediately.

Each serving About 347 calories, 14 g protein, 12 g carbohydrate, 29 g total fat (8 g saturated), 4 g fiber, 32 mg cholesterol, 400 mg sodium.

Moroccan Lamb Chops

From Redbook

Total time **15 minutes**

MAKES 4 MAIN-DISH SERVINGS

- 8 **loin lamb chops, 1-inch thick (5 oz. each)**
- ½ **cup bottled or homemade honey–Dijon vinaigrette**
- 1 **lemon, zested and juiced**
  Salt and pepper
  Fruity, Nutty Couscous and/or Carrot Coins (optional, see below)

1. Preheat indoor grill pan or broiler.
2. Place lamb chops in shallow dish. In bowl, whisk vinaigrette, 1 teaspoon lemon zest, 2 tablespoons lemon juice, 1 teaspoon salt, and ½ teaspoon freshly ground black pepper; pour over chops, turning to coat.
3. Grill or broil lamb 10 minutes, turning once for medium-rare. Serve with couscous and carrots, if desired.

Each serving without sides About 630 calories, 41 g protein, 7 g carbohydrate, 48 g total fat (18 g saturated), 0 g fiber, 164 mg cholesterol, 918 mg sodium.

FRUITY, NUTTY COUSCOUS

Cook 1 box (6.1 oz.) **curry couscous** according to package directions. Stir in ½ cup chopped dried **apricots,** ½ cup **pistachios,** and 2 tablespoons chopped **fresh mint** or parsley.

Each serving About 297 calories, 10 g protein, 47 g carbohydrate, 10 g total fat (1 g saturated), 5 g fiber, 0 mg cholesterol, 438 mg sodium.

CARROT COINS

In bowl, combine 1 tablespoon **olive oil,** 1 tablespoon **apple cider vinegar,** 2 teaspoons **honey,** ¼ teaspoon **salt,** and ¼ teaspoon ground **black pepper.** Add 6 ounces sliced **carrots;** toss.

Each serving About 59 calories, 0 g protein, 7 g carbohydrate, 3 g total fat (0 g saturated), 1 g fiber, 0 mg cholesterol, 175 mg sodium.

Bistro **Lamb Chops** with Sun-dried Tomato–Olive Butter

From Redbook

Total time **12 minutes**

MAKES 4 MAIN-DISH SERVINGS

- 2 **Tbsp. unsalted butter, softened**
- 1 **Tbsp. tapenade (olive paste)**
- 1 **Tbsp. sun-dried-tomato pesto**
- 4 **loin lamb chops, 1-inch thick (6 oz. each)**
- **Salt and pepper**

1. Preheat broiler. In bowl, combine butter, tapenade, and pesto.
2. Sprinkle lamb chops with ½ teaspoon salt and ¼ teaspoon freshly ground black pepper. Broil lamb 4 inches from heat source, 4 to 5 minutes per side, turning once for medium-rare. Remove from broiler. Spoon butter mixture onto each chop, dividing evenly.

Each serving About 383 calories, 25 g protein, 1 g carbohydrate, 30 g total fat (14 g saturated), 0 g fiber, 114 mg cholesterol, 428 mg sodium.

3 INGREDIENTS

MAKE IT A MEAL

Add steamed asparagus and mashed potatoes (see our yummy recipes on the next spread), and it's dinner!

Ultimate Mashed Potatoes

From Country Living

Active time **10 minutes**
Total time **40 minutes**

MAKES 6 SIDE-DISH SERVINGS

2½ lb. russet potatoes, peeled and cut into 2½-inch cubes

Kosher salt and pepper

4 Tbsp. unsalted butter, melted

¾ cup half-and-half, heated

1. In large pot, cover potatoes with salted water by 2 inches. Bring to boiling on medium-high. Reduce heat to medium, and simmer until potatoes are tender when pierced with knife, about 25 minutes.

2. Drain potatoes thoroughly; return to pot. Add melted butter and, using potato masher, mash potatoes to desired consistency. (For smoother texture, pass potatoes through ricer.)

3. Stir in half-and-half and 1 teaspoon salt to combine and until potatoes are creamy. Do not overstir or potatoes will become gluey. Season with salt and freshly ground black pepper; serve hot.

Each serving About 260 calories, 4 g protein, 37 g carbohydrate, 11 g total fat (7 g saturated), 3 g fiber, 31 mg cholesterol, 209 mg sodium.

4 Scrumptious Variations

Whip up the Ultimate Mashed Potatoes (opposite), then stir in one of these mouthwatering flavor combinations

1 Fried Shallots & Crème Fraîche

In medium skillet on medium-high, heat 4 tablespoons oil. Cook 3 large, sliced **shallots,** until golden, 6 to 8 minutes. (Discard any shallots that overbrown.) Using slotted spoon, transfer shallots to paper towel–lined plate and sprinkle with ¼ teaspoon **sea salt.** Stir shallots and ⅓ cup **crème fraîche** into mashed potatoes.

2 Horseradish, Sour Cream & Black Pepper

Stir ½ cup finely grated fresh **horseradish,** ½ cup **sour cream,** and freshly ground **black pepper** to taste into mashed potatoes.

3 Prosciutto, Parmesan & Parsley

Stir 3 ounces **prosciutto,** cooked and chopped; 6 tablespoons freshly grated **Parmesan;** and 3 tablespoons finely chopped **parsley** into mashed potatoes.

4 Roquefort, Walnuts & Sage

Stir 4 ounces **Roquefort cheese,** crumbled; ⅓ cup chopped **walnuts,** toasted; and 2 teaspoons chopped **sage** into mashed potatoes.

Healthy and delicious, fish can be ready in a flash. It's a great choice when time is short, but you still want to eat smart.

SPEEDY SEAFOOD

Roasted Halibut *with* Grapefruit Salsa

From Redbook

Total time **12 minutes**

MAKES 4 MAIN-DISH SERVINGS

- **2** large red or pink grapefruit
- **1** red Fresno or jalapeño chile, seeded and minced
- **3** Tbsp. diced red onion
- **2** Tbsp. slivered fresh basil leaves
- **1** tsp. chopped fresh thyme
- **4** halibut fillets, 1-inch thick (6 oz. each)
  Vegetable oil
  Salt and pepper

1. Preheat oven to 450°F. Cut away peel and pith from grapefruit. Cut segments into medium bowl; snip segments into smaller pieces, and squeeze juice from membranes into same bowl. Add chile, onion, basil, and thyme.
2. Line baking sheet with parchment paper or nonstick foil. Brush halibut with oil, and season with salt and freshly ground black pepper. Place on prepared baking sheet. Roast fish 10 to 12 minutes, until cooked through. To serve, spoon salsa over fish.

Each serving About 230 calories, 31 g protein, 13 g carbohydrate, 6 g total fat (1 g saturated), 2 g fiber, 81 mg cholesterol, 112 mg sodium.

SKINNY FISH
Only 230 calories per serving! And it's done in 12 minutes flat.

5 INGREDIENTS

Greek-Style
Tilapia

From Good Housekeeping

Active time **10 minutes**
Total time **25 minutes**

MAKES 4 MAIN-DISH SERVINGS

- 2 **lemons**
- 1½ **lb. tilapia fillets**
- 1 **Tbsp. chopped fresh oregano leaves, plus oregano sprigs for garnish**
  Salt and pepper
- 1 **pint grape tomatoes, each cut lengthwise in half**
- 8 **oz. orzo pasta**

1. Preheat oven to 400°F. From lemons, grate ½ teaspoon peel and squeeze ¼ cup juice.

2. In 13" by 9" glass or ceramic baking dish, arrange tilapia fillets. Evenly sprinkle fillets with lemon juice and peel, chopped oregano, ¼ teaspoon salt, and ¼ teaspoon freshly ground black pepper. Add tomatoes to baking dish around tilapia; cover with foil and roast 16 to 18 minutes or until tilapia is opaque throughout and tomatoes are tender.

3. Meanwhile, heat covered 4-quart saucepan of salted water to boiling on high. Add orzo and cook as label directs. Drain well.

4. Serve tilapia, tomatoes, and orzo with juices from baking dish.

Each serving About 395 calories, 36 g protein, 50 g carbohydrate, 6 g total fat (0 g saturated), 2 g fiber, 0 mg cholesterol, 310 mg sodium.

Striped Bass *with* Green Lentil Salad

From Redbook

Active time **15 minutes**
Total time **30 minutes**

MAKES 4 MAIN-DISH SERVINGS

- ⅔ cup French green lentils
- 1 red bell pepper, finely diced
- 1 small red onion, finely diced
- 3 Tbsp. extra virgin olive oil
  Kosher salt and pepper
- 4 thick skin-on striped bass fillets (6 oz. each)
- 2 limes, zested and juiced
- 3 Tbsp. unsalted butter
  Frisée leaves, for garnish (optional)

1. In medium saucepan, bring lentils and 6 cups water to boiling. Gently boil 15 minutes, or until lentils are just tender and still hold their shape; drain and transfer to large bowl. Add bell pepper, onion, 2 tablespoons oil, ½ teaspoon salt, and ¼ teaspoon freshly ground black pepper. Cover bowl and keep warm.

2. Sprinkle bass with ½ teaspoon salt and ¼ teaspoon pepper; on flesh side of fillets, rub 2 teaspoons lime zest.

3. Heat large nonstick skillet on medium-high for 2 minutes. Add 1 tablespoon oil, then place fillets, skin side down, in skillet. Cook fish 3 to 4 minutes, until skin is crisp. Turn

fish over, lower heat to medium-low, and cook 3 minutes longer, until almost cooked through (fish will begin to flake and separate a little, and center will be slightly translucent). Remove to plate.

4. To same skillet on high, add ¼ cup lime juice; bring to boiling. When juice is reduced by half, remove skillet from heat and swirl in butter, ½ teaspoon salt, and ¼ teaspoon pepper, until sauce is emulsified.

5. Line plates with frisée, if using. Top with lentil salad and fillets; spoon lime butter over each plate.

Each serving About 458 calories, 38 g protein, 24 g carbohydrate, 24 g total fat (8 g saturated), 6 g fiber, 159 mg cholesterol, 847 mg sodium.

5 INGREDIENTS

Arctic Char *with* Couscous & Roasted Asparagus

5 INGREDIENTS

FAST FRIENDS
Quick-cooking grains such as couscous are the perfect partners for speedy entrées like fish.

From Redbook

Active time **10 minutes**
Total time **30 minutes**

MAKES 4 MAIN-DISH SERVINGS

2½ Tbsp. olive oil

1¾ cups Israeli couscous

1 bunch (¾ lb.) pencil-thin
   asparagus, ends trimmed

4 sprigs fresh lemon thyme
   Kosher salt and pepper

4 skin-on arctic char fillets
   (6 oz. each)

1 Tbsp. capers, drained

1 Tbsp. unsalted butter
   Lemon wedges (optional)

1. Preheat oven to 350°F. In saucepan on medium-high, heat 1 tablespoon oil; add couscous and, stirring constantly, toast until light amber in color, about 2 minutes. Add 1¾ cups water, bring to boiling, reduce heat to low, cover, and simmer 8 to 10 minutes, until water has been absorbed and couscous is al dente. Fluff with fork.
2. Meanwhile, on baking sheet, toss asparagus and thyme with ½ tablespoon oil, ¼ teaspoon salt, and ¼ teaspoon freshly ground black pepper. Roast 10 minutes or until crisp-tender.
3. Pat fish dry; season with ¼ teaspoon salt and ¼ teaspoon pepper. In large nonstick skillet on medium-high, heat remaining oil until shimmering. Add fish to skillet, skin side down, and cook undisturbed for 3 minutes; turn fillets and cook until fish is just cooked through, about 2 to 3 minutes longer. With slotted spatula, transfer fish to large plate.
4. Deglaze skillet with ½ cup water, scraping up browned bits; add capers and butter, remove skillet from heat, and swirl until incorporated.
5. To serve, mound couscous on each plate and top with fish and roasted asparagus. Spoon caper sauce over fish. Serve with lemon wedges, if desired.

Each serving About 648 calories, 50 g protein, 51 g carbohydrate, 26 g total fat (7 g saturated), 4 g fiber, 53 mg cholesterol, 446 mg sodium.

Sicilian Swordfish

From Redbook

Total time **10 minutes**

MAKES 4 MAIN-DISH SERVINGS

4 swordfish steaks, 1-inch thick
   (6 oz. each)

2 Tbsp. extra virgin olive oil
   Salt and pepper

1 cup Sicilian eggplant-and-olive
   sauce or marinara sauce

1. Preheat oven to 400°F. Place fish in baking dish. Brush with olive oil; sprinkle with ¼ teaspoon salt and ¼ teaspoon freshly ground black pepper. Bake 5 minutes.
2. Pour sauce over fish; bake 5 minutes longer. If desired, serve with orzo and sautéed zucchini and yellow squash.

Each serving without sides About 353 calories, 34 g protein, 5 g carbohydrate, 21 g total fat (4 g saturated), 1 g fiber, 112 mg cholesterol, 543 mg sodium.

LIKE SALMON? Try arctic char. It's a close relative with a light flavor—and lots of omega-3 acids.

Provençale **Arctic Char**

From Redbook

Total time **15 minutes**

MAKES 4 MAIN-DISH SERVINGS

- **4 skin-on arctic char fillets (5 oz. each)**
- **Kosher salt and pepper**
- **3 Tbsp. olive oil**
- **1 zucchini (6 oz.), cut into ¼-inch-thick rounds**
- **1 yellow summer squash (6 oz.), cut into ¼-inch-thick rounds**
- **½ cup red and green Cerignola olives**
- **1 large ripe beefsteak tomato, cut into 1-inch chunks**
- **4 sprigs fresh tarragon, each about 4 inches long**
- **1 Tbsp. white balsamic vinegar**
- **1 lemon, cut into 4 wedges**

1. Season fish with ½ teaspoon salt and ¼ teaspoon freshly ground black pepper. In large nonstick skillet on medium, heat 1½ tablespoons oil until shimmering; add fillets, skin side down. Cook, undisturbed, for 3 minutes. Turn fillets; cook 3 minutes longer for medium doneness. Transfer fillets to serving plate.

2. Add remaining oil to same skillet; add zucchini, yellow squash, olives, tomato, and tarragon. Raise heat to high; cook 3 minutes or until squash is crisp-tender. Stir in vinegar, ¼ teaspoon salt, and ¼ teaspoon pepper; cook 1 minute.

3. Spoon vegetable mixture onto platter and top with fillets. Serve with lemon wedges.

Each serving About 439 calories, 37 g protein, 9 g carbohydrate, 29 g total fat (5 g saturated), 2 g fiber, 38 mg cholesterol, 958 mg sodium.

Tandoori Shrimp

From Redbook

Total time **15 minutes**

MAKES 4 MAIN-DISH SERVINGS

- 1 **lb. large shrimp, shelled and deveined**
- ½ **cup fat-free plain Greek yogurt**
- 1 **Tbsp. fresh lime juice**
- 2 **tsp. curry powder**
- 2 **tsp. garlic paste**
  Kosher salt
- 1 **onion, thinly sliced**

1. Pat shrimp dry. In medium bowl, combine shrimp, yogurt, lime juice, curry powder, garlic paste, and salt to taste.

2. Preheat indoor grill pan. Add onion, and cook about 8 minutes or until lightly browned. Remove to plate.

3. Add shrimp to grill, and cook until shrimp are cooked through, 2 to 3 minutes. If desired, serve with jasmine rice, mango chutney, and lime wedges.

Each serving without sides About 118 calories, 19 g protein, 7 g carbohydrate, 1 g total fat (0 g saturated), 1 g fiber, 143 mg cholesterol, 690 mg sodium.

DOUBLE PEA & FETA SALAD

From Redbook

Total time **15 minutes**

MAKES 6 SIDE-DISH SERVINGS

Bring large saucepan of lightly salted water to boiling; add 1 pound sugar snap peas (stems and strings removed) and 1 bag (1 pound) frozen green peas. When water returns to boiling, cook 1½ to 2 minutes, until sugar snaps are crisp-tender. Drain; refresh under cold running water. Drain peas well (blot with a paper towel). In large serving bowl, toss peas with ¼ cup thinly sliced red onions; ¼ cup fresh mint leaves, slivered; 2½ tablespoons extra virgin olive oil; and kosher salt and freshly ground black pepper, to taste. Gently stir in ¾ cup crumbled feta cheese and ¼ cup toasted pine nuts (optional).

Each serving without pine nuts About 190 calories, 8 g protein, 17 g carbohydrate, 10 g total fat (4 g saturated), 6 g fiber, 17 mg cholesterol, 304 mg sodium.

Grilled Scallops *with* Citrus Salsa

From Redbook

Total time **15 minutes**

MAKES 4 MAIN-DISH SERVINGS

- 2 **red grapefruit, peeled**
- 2 **oranges, peeled**
- 1 **Tbsp. fresh lime juice**
- ¼ **cup chopped red onion**
- 2 **Tbsp. chopped fresh cilantro leaves**
- 1 **lb. sea scallops**
- 1 **Tbsp. olive oil**
  Coarse salt

1. Over medium bowl, cut grapefruit into segments and remove membranes; halve each segment. Repeat with oranges, but leave segments whole. Add lime juice, onion, cilantro, and ½ teaspoon salt, tossing to combine. **2.** Preheat outdoor grill or heat indoor grill pan to medium-high. Toss scallops in oil and sprinkle with ½ teaspoon salt. Grill 4 to 6 minutes, flipping halfway through, until opaque. **3.** Serve scallops with citrus salsa.

Each serving About 280 calories, 33 g protein, 28 g carbohydrate, 5 g total fat (1 g saturated), 3 g fiber, 77 mg cholesterol, 849 mg sodium.

Thai **Basil Shrimp**

From Redbook

Total time 10 minutes

MAKES 4 MAIN-DISH SERVINGS

- **3 shallots, thinly sliced**
- **2 tsp. chopped garlic**
- **1–2 sliced red or green chiles**
- **2 Tbsp. fish sauce**
- **1 Tbsp. soy sauce**
- **1 Tbsp. lime juice**
- **2 tsp. brown sugar**
- **½ cup fresh Thai or regular basil leaves**
- **2 Tbsp. vegetable or peanut oil**
- **1 lb. large shrimp, peeled (tails left on) and deveined**

1. In small bowl, combine shallots, garlic, and chiles. In another bowl, combine fish sauce, soy sauce, lime juice, brown sugar, and basil.
2. In large skillet on medium-high, heat oil; add shallot mixture and cook until garlic is lightly golden, 1 minute. Add shrimp; stir-fry 1 minute. Add soy sauce mixture; stir-fry until shrimp are just cooked through, 2 to 3 minutes. Serve over jasmine rice, if desired.

Each serving without rice About 141 calories, 13 g protein, 7 g carbohydrate, 8 g total fat (1 g saturated), 0 g fiber, 114 mg cholesterol, 1,173 mg sodium.

QUICK PICK
Ordering takeout
is fast—but this recipe
is even faster.

GOOD FOR YOU!
Salmon plus
ginger plus veggies
makes healthy
taste great.

5 INGREDIENTS

Ginger Salmon Skewers *with* Asian Slaw

From Redbook

Total time **12 minutes**

MAKES 4 MAIN-DISH SERVINGS

- 1 **small bunch fresh cilantro**
- 4 **skinless salmon fillets, 1-inch thick (6 oz. each)**
- 2 **Tbsp. vegetable oil**
- 2 **Tbsp. soy sauce**
- 1 **Tbsp. grated fresh ginger**
- 1 **Tbsp. fresh lime juice**
- ½ **tsp. sugar**
- 4 **cups shredded Napa cabbage**
- 1 **cup shredded carrots**
- ½ **cup sliced radishes**
- 1 **minced shallot**
  Rice vinegar
  Salt and pepper

1. From bunch of cilantro, mince 2 tablespoons and chop ½ cup.
2. Cut salmon into large cubes and thread on skewers. In medium bowl, whisk oil, minced cilantro, soy sauce, ginger, lime juice, and sugar until well combined; brush over salmon.
3. In large bowl, toss together cabbage, carrots, radishes, shallot, and chopped cilantro. Season with rice vinegar, salt, and freshly ground black pepper to taste.
4. Preheat indoor grill pan. Cook salmon 2 to 3 minutes per side (for medium). Serve skewers with slaw.

Each serving About 379 calories, 41 g protein, 8 g carbohydrate, 19 g total fat (2 g saturated), 2 g fiber, 107 mg cholesterol, 572 mg sodium.

Roasted Salmon *with* Summer Squash

From Good Housekeeping

Active time **15 minutes**
Total time **30 minutes**

MAKES 4 MAIN-DISH SERVINGS

- 1 **lemon**
- 4 **skinless salmon fillets (6 oz. each)**
  Salt and pepper
- 2 **medium yellow squash (8 oz. each), cut into ½-inch-thick slices**
- 2 **medium zucchini (8 oz. each), cut into ½-inch-thick slices**
- 1 **Tbsp. chopped fresh tarragon leaves plus sprigs for garnish**

1. Preheat oven to 400°F. From lemon, grate ½ teaspoon peel and squeeze 3 tablespoons juice.
2. Place salmon in 13" by 9" glass or ceramic baking dish. Sprinkle with lemon zest, 1 tablespoon lemon juice, ¼ teaspoon salt, and ⅛ teaspoon freshly ground black pepper. Roast 14 to 16 minutes or until just opaque.
3. Meanwhile, place steamer basket and 1 inch water in 4-quart saucepan. Heat water to boiling. Add squash and zucchini; cover and reduce heat to medium. Steam vegetables 8 minutes or until tender. Transfer to bowl; toss with remaining 2 tablespoons lemon juice, chopped tarragon, ¼ teaspoon salt, and ⅛ teaspoon freshly ground black pepper. Arrange vegetables and salmon on plates; garnish with tarragon sprigs.

Each serving About 275 calories, 37 g protein, 8 g carbohydrate, 11 g total fat (2 g saturated), 3 g fiber, 93 mg cholesterol, 375 mg sodium.

ZUCCHINI RIBBONS with LEMON & GARLIC

From Redbook

Total time **5 minutes**

MAKES 6 SIDE-DISH SERVINGS

With vegetable peeler, cut 4 medium **zucchini** into long, thin ribbons. In

large skillet, melt 2 tablespoons **butter.** Add zucchini, 1 **garlic clove,** grated; and 1 teaspoon grated **lemon zest.** Cook, stirring, until tender, 2 minutes. Sprinkle with 2 teaspoons minced fresh **tarragon.** Season to taste with **salt** and freshly ground **black pepper.**

Each serving About 49 calories, 1 g protein, 3 g carbohydrate, 4 g total fat (2 g saturated), 1 g fiber, 10 mg cholesterol, 37 mg sodium.

4 INGREDIENTS

Salmon Pilaf *with* Green Onions

From Good Housekeeping

Active time **10 minutes**
Total time **30 minutes**

MAKES 4 MAIN-DISH SERVINGS

- 1¼ **cups long-grain white rice**
- 1 **bunch green onions (about 6)**
- 1 **Tbsp. olive oil**
- 1 **lb. skinless salmon fillet, cut into 1-inch chunks**
  Pepper
- ¼ **cup teriyaki sauce**

1. Prepare rice as label directs, without salt. Thinly slice onions; reserve 2 tablespoons of the dark green slices for garnishing pilaf.
2. Meanwhile, in 12-inch nonstick skillet on medium, heat oil 1 minute. Add onions and cook 3 minutes, stirring occasionally. Season salmon with ⅛ teaspoon freshly ground black pepper. Add salmon to skillet, and cook 7 to 8 minutes or until opaque throughout, stirring occasionally. Remove skillet from heat; discard any fat, but leave salmon in skillet.
3. Stir cooked rice and teriyaki sauce into skillet with salmon until well blended. To serve, garnish with dark green onion slices.

Each serving About 410 calories, 28 g protein, 51 g carbohydrate, 9 g total fat (1 g saturated), 1 g fiber, 62 mg cholesterol, 745 mg sodium.

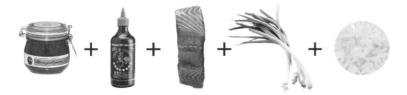

Spicy Glazed
Salmon

From Country Living

Active time **10 minutes**
Total time **20 minutes**

MAKES 4 MAIN-DISH SERVINGS

- ⅓ cup peach preserves
- 1½ tsp. chile sauce, preferably Sriracha
- 4 skin-on salmon fillets (6 oz. each)
- 3 green onions
- 2 cups rice, cooked

1. Prepare outdoor grill or heat indoor grill pan on medium heat until hot. Heat grill to medium in 1 zone and medium-low in another. To make glaze: In microwave-safe dish, microwave preserves until just warmed, 10 to 15 seconds. Stir in chile sauce. Transfer all but 3 tablespoons of mixture to small bowl; set aside bowl of glaze to serve at the table.

2. Season salmon fillets with salt. Grill fillets, skin side down, on medium heat zone for about 10 minutes. Meanwhile, grill onions on medium-low zone until sear marks appear, about 3 minutes. Remove onions, chop, and stir into rice; set aside and keep warm.

3. Brush fillets with some peach glaze. Using metal spatula, flip each piece. Continue to grill until flesh is cooked, 2 to 3 more minutes. Remove and brush with more glaze. Serve salmon over rice and with reserved bowl of glaze.

Each serving About 528 calories, 37 g protein, 41 g carbohydrate, 23 g total fat (2 g saturated), 1 g fiber, 94 mg cholesterol, 160 mg sodium.

5 INGREDIENTS

Spaghetti, tortellini, and other pastas headline in these recipes that deliver flavor-packed meals pronto!

PASTA
PRESTO

Pasta *with* Tomatoes, Basil & Olives

From Redbook

Total time **15 minutes**

MAKES 6 MAIN-DISH SERVINGS

- Salt
- 1 **lb. campanelle or farfalle pasta**
- 1½ **lb. plum tomatoes, cut into ½-inch chunks**
- 6 **oz. ricotta salata or feta cheese, crumbled**
- ½ **cup pitted niçoise or kalamata olives**
- ½ **cup torn fresh basil leaves**
- ¼ **cup extra virgin olive oil**
- 2 **oz. shaved Parmesan cheese**

1. Heat large covered saucepot of salted water to boiling on high. Add pasta and cook as label directs. Drain pasta and return to saucepot.

2. Meanwhile, in large serving bowl, toss tomatoes, ricotta salata, olives, basil, and oil.

3. Add tomato mixture to pasta, tossing to combine. Top with shaved Parmesan cheese.

Each serving About 578 calories, 17 g protein, 71 g carbohydrate, 25 g total fat (9 g saturated), 4 g fiber, 37 mg cholesterol, 776 mg sodium.

GREAT SHAPE
Campanelle pasta looks
like small bells.

5 INGREDIENTS

SAUCE SECRET
Soft and rich mascarpone makes this pasta dish creamy—and delicious.

Lemon Pasta *with* Squash & Pancetta

From Redbook

Total time **15 minutes**

MAKES 4 MAIN-DISH SERVINGS

Salt and pepper

12 oz. **tagliatelle or fettuccine pasta**

1 cup **mascarpone cheese, softened**

1 **lemon, zested and juiced**

2 tsp. **olive oil**

2 oz. **thinly sliced pancetta**

1 lb. **small-to-medium summer squash (zucchini and yellow squash), thinly sliced**

1 Tbsp. **unsalted butter, softened**

Freshly grated Parmesan cheese (optional)

1. Heat large covered saucepot of salted water to boiling. Add pasta and cook as label directs.

2. Meanwhile, in large serving bowl, combine mascarpone, 2 teaspoons lemon zest, 2 tablespoons lemon juice, ½ teaspoon salt, and ½ teaspoon freshly ground black pepper; set aside.

3. In skillet on medium, heat oil; add pancetta and cook until crisp, about 4 minutes. Drain on paper towels. Add squash to drippings in skillet. Cook 2 minutes or until just tender, then scatter squash over top of mascarpone mixture. Cover bowl with foil to keep warm.

4. Drain pasta, reserving ½ cup pasta cooking water. Add pasta, butter, and half of the reserved cooking water to bowl; gently toss until pasta is evenly coated, adding more cooking water if needed. Crumble reserved pancetta in large pieces over pasta; toss. Serve with grated Parmesan cheese, if desired.

Each serving without cheese About 700 calories, 18 g protein, 68 g carbohydrate, 41 g total fat (20 g saturated), 4 g fiber, 93 mg cholesterol, 534 mg sodium.

Tortellini Toss *with* Herbed Goat Cheese

From Good Housekeeping

Total time **15 minutes**

MAKES 4 MAIN-DISH SERVINGS

   Salt

2 **packages (9 oz. each) refrigerated cheese tortellini**

1 **bag (5 oz.) baby spinach**

½ **tsp. lemon zest**

¼ **cup oil-packed sun-dried tomatoes, drained and chopped (reserve 1 Tbsp. oil from jar)**

2 **oz. herbed goat cheese, crumbled**

1. Heat large covered saucepot of salted water to boiling. Cook tortellini as label directs. Reserve ¼ cup pasta cooking water; drain tortellini and return to saucepot with reserved cooking water.
2. Stir in spinach, lemon zest, and sun-dried tomatoes and their oil; toss to coat. Transfer to serving bowls and sprinkle with goat cheese.

Each serving About 485 calories, 23 g protein, 60 g carbohydrate, 16 g total fat (7 g saturated), 9 g fiber, 77 mg cholesterol, 880 mg sodium.

EVEN *MORE* PRESTO PASTA!

Our delicious pasta recipes are really fast, but there's a way to get them ready even faster:
Use fresh pasta! Dried pasta cooks in about 8 to 12 minutes after the water has returned to boiling, but fresh pasta can be done in as few as 1 to 3 minutes—or up to 7 minutes, if it's stuffed, like tortellini. Fresh noodles are finer textured and richer, because they're made with eggs. They pair best with delicate sauces. Dried pasta, made from flour and water, is cheaper and lower in fat, and works well with strongly flavored sauces.

5 INGREDIENTS

4 INGREDIENTS

Pasta *with* Sausage & Broccoli Rabe

From Country Living

Total time **25 minutes**

MAKES 6 MAIN-DISH SERVINGS

- 12 oz. Italian chicken sausage
- 2 Tbsp. olive oil
  Salt
- 1 large bunch broccoli rabe (about 1½ lb.), trimmed and cut into 2½-inch pieces
- ½ lb. cavatelli or orechiette pasta
- 4 medium garlic cloves, chopped

1. In large skillet on medium-low, place sausage and ½ cup water. Cover and simmer for 10 minutes; drain. Cut sausage into ⅓-inch-thick slices. Heat oil in same skillet on medium-high. Add sausage and cook until browned, about 6 minutes, turning once. Transfer to plate, reserving oil.

2. Meanwhile, heat large covered saucepot of salted water to boiling on high. Add broccoli rabe, and cook until leaves are wilted, 1 to 2 minutes. With slotted spoon, transfer broccoli rabe to colander and drain. Return water to boiling. Add pasta and cook as label directs.

3. In same skillet on medium-high, add broccoli rabe and garlic. Cook until broccoli rabe is tender, about 4 minutes. Return sausage to skillet and reduce heat to low.

4. Reserve ½ cup pasta cooking water; drain pasta and return to saucepot. Stir reserved cooking water into skillet, scraping up browned bits from bottom. Toss pasta with broccoli rabe; serve immediately.

Each serving About 250 calories, 17 g protein, 20 g carbohydrate, 7 g total fat (2 g saturated), 1 g fiber, 48 mg cholesterol, 374 mg sodium.

Farfalle *with* Sausage & Arugula

From Redbook

Total time **15 minutes**

MAKES 4 MAIN-DISH SERVINGS

Salt

¾ lb. farfalle pasta

1 Tbsp. olive oil

1 lb. Italian chicken sausage, casings removed, crumbled

4 jarred roasted red and yellow peppers, cut into thin strips

8 oz. baby arugula or spinach, stems trimmed

½ tsp. crushed red pepper flakes

¼ cup freshly grated Parmesan cheese

1. Heat large covered saucepot of salted water to boiling on high. Add pasta and cook as label directs. Reserve 1 cup pasta cooking water; drain pasta and return to saucepot.

2. Meanwhile, in large skillet on medium, heat oil. Add sausage and cook until meat is no longer pink, about 4 minutes. Add peppers, stirring to combine. Add arugula in batches, stirring until each batch is wilted before adding the next.

3. Add sausage mixture, red pepper flakes, and some of the reserved cooking water to pasta, and toss to combine.

4. Divide among 4 bowls; sprinkle with Parmesan cheese.

Each serving About 590 calories, 31 g protein, 80 g carbohydrate, 15 g total fat (4 g saturated), 4 g fiber, 93 mg cholesterol, 1,080 mg sodium.

Rotini *with* Shrimp & Bacon

From Good Housekeeping

Total time **20 minutes**

MAKES 4 MAIN-DISH SERVINGS

Salt

12 oz. rotini pasta

4 slices bacon, cut crosswise into ½-inch strips

1 lb. large shrimp, shelled and deveined

½ cup fresh basil leaves, thinly sliced, plus additional leaves for garnish

2 lemons, zested and juiced

1. Heat large covered saucepot of salted water to boiling on high. Add pasta and cook as label directs. Reserve ½ cup pasta cooking water; drain pasta and return to saucepot.

2. Meanwhile, in 12-inch nonstick skillet, cook bacon on medium 9 to 10 minutes or until crisp and golden. With slotted spoon, transfer bacon to paper towel–lined plate to drain. Remove all but 1 tablespoon bacon fat from skillet.

3. To same skillet, add shrimp; cook on medium 4 minutes, stirring often. Stir in reserved cooking water, and heat to boiling on medium. Cook 1 to 2 minutes or until shrimp are opaque throughout. Remove from heat; stir in basil, ½ teaspoon lemon zest, ¼ cup lemon juice, and reserved bacon. Add shrimp mixture to pasta and toss to coat. Transfer to bowls and garnish with basil leaves.

Each serving About 505 calories, 36 g protein, 66 g carbohydrate, 10 g total fat (3 g saturated), 2 g fiber, 181 mg cholesterol, 420 mg sodium.

5 INGREDIENTS

15 MINUTES

Gemelli *with* Asparagus & Pancetta

From Redbook
Total time **15 minutes**

MAKES 6 MAIN-DISH SERVINGS

- **Salt and pepper**
- 1 **lb. thin asparagus, trimmed and cut diagonally into 2-inch pieces**
- 1 **lb. gemelli pasta**
- 3 **Tbsp. olive oil**
- 4 **oz. sliced pancetta, slices cut into thin strips and separated**
- 1 **orange bell pepper, cut into strips**
- ½ **cup shaved Grana Padano or Parmesan cheese, plus extra for serving**

1. Heat large covered saucepot of salted water to boiling on high. Add asparagus; blanch 1 minute, or until bright green. Scoop asparagus from water with handheld strainer and refresh under cold water.

2. Bring water back to boiling; add pasta and cook as label directs.

3. Meanwhile, heat oil in large, deep skillet on medium. Add pancetta and cook, stirring frequently, until crisp and most of the fat has been rendered, about 7 minutes. Add asparagus and pepper, and continue to cook 1 to 2 minutes, tossing, until vegetables are crisp-tender. Remove from heat.

4. Drain pasta, reserving ½ cup pasta cooking water. Add pasta and freshly ground black pepper to taste to skillet; toss until combined. Add cheese and reserved cooking water, and toss well. Serve immediately with extra cheese, if desired.

Each serving without extra cheese About 455 calories, 15 g protein, 60 g carbohydrate, 17 g total fat (5 g saturated), 4 g fiber, 14 mg cholesterol, 327 mg sodium.

Spaghetti
alla Carbonara

From Redbook

Total time **15 minutes**

MAKES 6 MAIN-DISH SERVINGS

   Salt
1 **lb. spaghetti**
2 **Tbsp. olive oil**
4 **oz. slab bacon or pancetta, cut into ¼-inch dice**
3 **extra large eggs**
¼ **cup chopped fresh flat-leaf parsley**
¼ **tsp. crushed red pepper flakes**
½ **cup grated Parmesan cheese**

1. Heat large covered saucepot of salted water to boiling on high. Add pasta and cook as label directs. Reserve 1 cup pasta cooking water; drain pasta and return to saucepot.

2. Meanwhile, in large, deep skillet on medium, heat oil. Add bacon, and cook 8 to 10 minutes, until bacon is golden brown and most of the fat has been rendered; remove skillet from heat.

3. In medium bowl, whisk eggs, parsley, ¼ teaspoon salt, and red pepper flakes until combined.

4. Add drained pasta to same skillet and toss well on medium-low until pasta is coated. Add egg mixture and some of the reserved cooking water; toss gently until spaghetti looks creamy. Add Parmesan cheese, and toss to combine. Serve immediately.

Each serving About 496 calories, 23 g protein, 58 g carbohydrate, 19 g total fat (5 g saturated), 3 g fiber, 126 mg cholesterol, 764 mg sodium.

5 INGREDIENTS

In the mood for lighter fare? Try a main-dish salad. You'll load up on veggies, save on calories, and have dinner ready right away!

SALADS
IN A SNAP

Shrimp Cocktail Salad

From Good Housekeeping

Total time **15 minutes**

MAKES 4 MAIN-DISH SERVINGS

- 4 **large ripe tomatoes, sliced**
- ¼ **cup prepared horseradish**
- 2 **tsp. packed brown sugar**
- 3 **Tbsp. extra virgin olive oil**
- 1 **Tbsp. fresh lemon juice**
- 1 **tsp. hot pepper sauce (such as Tabasco)**
- **Salt and pepper**
- 4 **stalks celery, thinly sliced, plus celery leaves for garnish**
- 1 **lb. cooked jumbo shrimp, shelled and deveined, with tail part of shell left on, if you like**

1. Set fine-mesh sieve over medium bowl. Holding 1 tomato slice over sieve, scoop seeds into sieve. Repeat with remaining slices. Press seeds in sieve to extract as much juice as possible; discard seeds. Divide tomato slices among plates.

2. Prepare dressing: Into bowl with tomato juice, whisk horseradish, sugar, oil, lemon juice, hot sauce, ⅛ teaspoon salt, and ⅛ teaspoon freshly ground black pepper until sugar dissolves.

3. To serve, arrange celery slices, then shrimp, over sliced tomatoes. Stir dressing to blend, then drizzle over salads; garnish with celery leaves.

Each serving **About 255 calories, 26 g protein, 13 g carbohydrate, 12 g total fat (2 g saturated), 3 g fiber, 221 mg cholesterol, 400 mg sodium.**

LIGHT & LUXE
Shrimp makes
a salad extra special.

Grilled Shrimp & White Bean Salad

From Redbook

Total time **10 minutes**

MAKES 4 MAIN-DISH SERVINGS

- **1** lb. large shrimp, shelled and deveined
- **2** Tbsp. olive oil
- **2** garlic cloves, chopped
  Kosher salt and pepper
- **3** cups white kidney beans (cannellini), rinsed and drained
- **1** lemon, zested and juiced
- **1** cup cherry tomatoes, halved
  Fresh watercress or arugula

1. Pat shrimp dry; toss with 1 tablespoon oil, half of the garlic, and salt and freshly ground black pepper to taste.

2. In medium saucepan on medium, heat remaining 1 tablespoon oil. Add remaining garlic; cook, stirring, about 1 minute. Add beans, reduce heat to low, and cover; cook, until warm, 4 to 5 minutes.

3. Meanwhile in indoor grill pan, cook shrimp until lightly browned and cooked through, 2 to 3 minutes.

4. In large bowl, combine shrimp, beans, 1 tablespoon lemon juice, ½ teaspoon lemon zest, tomatoes, and salt and pepper to taste. Serve salad on top of fresh watercress or arugula drizzled with a little olive oil, if desired.

Each serving About 300 calories, 23 g protein, 30 g carbohydrate, 9 g total fat (1 g saturated), 8 g fiber, 143 mg cholesterol,

5 INGREDIENTS

Shrimp, Watermelon & Feta Salad

From Good Housekeeping

Total time **10 minutes**

MAKES 4 MAIN-DISH SERVINGS

- ¼ cup bottled lemon-and-chive dressing
- 1 lb. large shrimp, shelled and deveined
- 1 bag (5 to 6 oz.) mixed baby greens
- 3 cups diced (½-inch chunks) seedless watermelon
- 2 oz. crumbled feta cheese

1. In 12-inch nonstick skillet on medium, heat 1 tablespoon dressing 1 minute. Add shrimp, and cook 6 to 8 minutes or until shrimp are opaque throughout, stirring occasionally.
2. Meanwhile, in bowl, toss greens, watermelon, and remaining 3 table-spoons dressing until evenly coated. To serve, divide salad among plates, and top with shrimp and crumbled feta.

Each serving About 280 calories, 27 g protein, 12 g carbohydrate, 14 g total fat (3 g saturated), 1 g fiber, 185 mg cholesterol, 415 mg sodium.

**FROM
THE PANTRY**
Just add a few fresh
ingredients to ones
you have on
hand, and this salad
is done!

Tuscan Tuna Salad

From Redbook

Total time **10 minutes**

MAKES 4 MAIN-DISH SERVINGS

- 1 **can (15 oz.) white kidney beans (cannellini), rinsed and drained**
- ½ **cup thinly sliced red onions**
- 1 **can (6 oz.) tuna in olive oil (drain; reserve oil)**
- 1 **cup diced plum tomatoes**
- ½ **cup pitted kalamata olives**
- 2 **Tbsp. chopped fresh flat-leaf parsley**
- 1 **lemon, zested and juiced**
  Salt and pepper
- 2 **cups torn arugula**
- 4 **thick flatbreads**

1. In bowl, combine beans, onions, tuna, tomatoes, olives, parsley, 2 tablespoons reserved tuna-can oil, 1 tablespoon lemon juice, ½ teaspoon lemon zest, ¼ teaspoon salt, and ¼ teaspoon freshly ground black pepper, tossing gently. Stir in arugula.
2. Preheat outdoor grill or indoor grill pan. Brush flatbreads lightly with the remaining reserved tuna-can oil. Grill until lightly browned, about 2 minutes per side. Cut flatbreads in halves or quarters. Serve with salad.

Each serving About 480 calories, 31 g protein, 51 g carbohydrate, 16 g total fat (3 g saturated), 7 g fiber, 27 mg cholesterol, 1,273 mg sodium.

California Roll Salad

From Good Housekeeping

Total time **15 minutes**

MAKES 4 MAIN-DISH SERVINGS

- 1 **package (8.8 oz.) precooked white rice in microwavable cups**
- 3 **Tbsp. seasoned light rice vinegar**
- 1 **head Boston lettuce**
- 1 **seedless cucumber, unpeeled and thinly sliced**
- 1 **ripe avocado, thinly sliced**
- 1 **lb. surimi (imitation crabmeat), broken into 1-inch chunks**
- 3 **Tbsp. lower-sodium soy sauce**
- 2 **Tbsp. slivered pickled ginger**

1. Prepare rice as label directs. Pour rice into medium bowl, and toss with 1 tablespoon vinegar; set aside.
2. Arrange lettuce leaves on large platter. Top leaves with seasoned rice, cucumber, avocado, and surimi.
3. In cup, combine soy sauce and remaining 2 tablespoons vinegar.
4. To serve, drizzle dressing over salad; sprinkle ginger on top.

Each serving About 310 calories, 18 g protein, 42 g carbohydrate, 9 g total fat (2 g saturated), 3 g fiber, 23 mg cholesterol, 1,685 mg sodium.

California Cobb Salad

From Redbook

Total time **15 minutes**

MAKES 6 MAIN-DISH SERVINGS

- ½ **cup bottled blue cheese dressing**
- ¾ **cup crumbled blue cheese**
- 1 **lemon, zested and juiced**
- 12 **cups shredded romaine lettuce**
- 2 **cups diced cooked chicken**
- 2 **cups diced cooked roast beef**
- 1 **cup diced zucchini**
- 1 **ripe avocado, diced**
- 4 **plum tomatoes, diced**
- 2 **hard-cooked eggs, chopped**
- 4 **oz. thick-sliced bacon, cut into ½-inch pieces, cooked**

1. Prepare lemon–blue cheese dressing: In small bowl, combine bottled dressing, ¼ cup blue cheese, 1 tablespoon lemon juice, and ½ teaspoon lemon zest.

2. In large bowl, toss lettuce with ¼ cup lemon–blue cheese dressing, and place on large platter. Arrange remaining ingredients on top of lettuce. Serve remaining dressing on the side.

Each serving About 406 calories, 31 g protein, 9 g carbohydrate, 28 g total fat (8 g saturated), 4 g fiber, 147 mg cholesterol, 900 mg sodium.

Smoked Turkey Salad

From Redbook

Active time **7 minutes**
Total time **12 minutes**

MAKES 4 MAIN-DISH SERVINGS

- ¼ cup slivered almonds
- 1 box (10 oz.) plain couscous
- ¾ lb. smoked turkey, diced
- 1½ cups cherry tomatoes, halved or quartered
- ½ cup pitted kalamata olives, sliced
- ½ cup bottled or homemade Greek salad dressing
- ¼ cup chopped fresh flat-leaf parsley

1. In dry medium skillet on medium, toast almonds, stirring frequently, until lightly browned, 4 to 5 minutes. Remove from heat.
2. In medium saucepan, cook couscous according to package directions.
3. Add couscous to large bowl with turkey, tomatoes, olives, dressing, and parsley; toss to combine. Serve turkey salad on top of fresh arugula or spinach, if desired.

Each serving without greens About 554 calories, 23 g protein, 87 g carbohydrate, 20 g total fat (2 g saturated), 5 g fiber, 38 mg cholesterol, 1,427 mg sodium.

Steak & Mushroom Salad

From Redbook

Active time **20 minutes**
Total time **30 minutes**

MAKES 4 MAIN-DISH SERVINGS

5 INGREDIENTS

- ½ **cup bottled or homemade red-wine or sherry vinaigrette**
- 1 **flank steak (1 lb.)**
- 12 **oz. cremini mushrooms, wiped clean and thinly sliced**
- 1 **bag (5 oz.) baby spinach**
- 6 **oz. Gorgonzola cheese, crumbled**

1. Place 3 tablespoons vinaigrette in large food-storage bag; add steak. Seal bag; toss to coat steak.

2. Into bowl, pour remaining 5 tablespoons vinaigrette. Add mushrooms; toss to coat in dressing. Scatter spinach on top of mushrooms; do not toss.

3. Preheat outdoor or indoor grill pan until very hot. Remove steak from bag and place on hot grill. Cook 5 minutes per side, or until internal temperature registers 135°F on instant-read thermometer for medium-rare. Transfer steak to cutting board; let steak rest 10 minutes. Thinly slice steak across the grain on slight diagonal.

4. Toss mushrooms and spinach in bowl; top with sliced steak. Garnish with Gorgonzola cheese.

Each serving About 431 calories, 36 g protein, 11 g carbohydrate, 27 g total fat (13 g saturated), 4 g fiber, 105 mg cholesterol, 1,009 mg sodium.

No-Cook Thai Beef Salad

From Good Housekeeping
Total time **15 minutes**
MAKES 4 MAIN-DISH SERVINGS

- 2 **limes, zested and juiced**
- 3 **Tbsp. lower-sodium fish sauce**
- 1 **Tbsp. sugar**
- 1 **bag (10 oz.) romaine salad mix**
- 1 **seedless cucumber, thinly sliced**
- 8 **oz. deli-sliced rare roast beef, cut into ½-inch-wide strips**
- 1 **cup fresh cilantro or mint leaves**
- ½ **medium red onion, thinly sliced**

1. Prepare dressing: in small bowl, combine 1 teaspoon lime zest, 3 tablespoons lime juice, fish sauce, and sugar; stir dressing until sugar is completely dissolved.

2. In large bowl, combine salad mix, cucumber, roast beef, cilantro, and onion. Add dressing to bowl, and toss. Divide salad among dinner plates.

Each serving About 105 calories, 13 g protein, 9 g carbohydrate, 2 g total fat (1 g saturated), 2 g fiber, 26 mg cholesterol, 485 mg sodium.

Pizza. Tacos. Quesadillas. Forget about takeout and make these treats at home in less time than it takes for delivery.

FAST
FUN FOOD

Taleggio, Prosciutto & Arugula **Pizza**

From Redbook

Total time **15 minutes**

MAKES 4 MAIN-DISH SERVINGS

- **1 lb. store-bought or homemade pizza dough**
- **1 small red onion, thinly sliced**
- **12 pitted oil-cured olives, halved**
- **¼ cup pine nuts**
- **3 Tbsp. olive oil**
- **8 oz. thinly sliced Taleggio cheese (rind removed)**
- **4 cups baby arugula**
- **4 slices prosciutto**
- **Pepper**

1. Place large pizza stone (or large heavy baking sheet) on lowest rack of oven; preheat oven to 500°F. On lightly floured 15-inch sheet nonstick foil or parchment paper, using rolling pin, roll out and stretch pizza dough into irregularly shaped 15″ by 12″ rectangle. Lightly prick dough all over with fork; top with onion, olives, and pine nuts. Drizzle with 2 tablespoons oil. Using cookie sheet or pizza peel, transfer dough from foil or parchment onto hot baking sheet. Bake 8 minutes, or until top is puffed and light golden. Remove from oven.

2. Top with Taleggio; bake 3 minutes longer, until cheese is just softened. Remove from oven.

3. In medium bowl, toss arugula with 2 teaspoons oil. Top pizza with salad. Place prosciutto over salad; top with remaining teaspoon olive oil and freshly ground black pepper.

Each serving About 650 calories, 27 g protein, 57 g carbohydrate, 37 g total fat (13 g saturated), 1 g fiber, 56 mg cholesterol, 1,804 mg sodium.

5 INGREDIENTS

Sausage & Pepper **Pizza**

From Redbook
Active time **15 minutes**
Total time **25 minutes**

MAKES 4 MAIN-DISH SERVINGS

- **4 hot and/or sweet Italian sausage links (about 10 oz. total)**
- **1 Tbsp. olive oil**
- **2 red and/or yellow bell peppers, seeded and cut into strips**
  Pepper
- **1 lb. frozen pizza dough, thawed**
- **¾ cup marinara or pizza sauce**
- **8 oz. shredded mozzarella cheese**
  Freshly grated Parmesan cheese (optional)

1. Preheat oven to 500°F. Cut sausages into ½-inch-thick slices. In large skillet on medium-high, heat oil; add sausages. Cook 4 minutes, tossing several times, until no longer pink on the outside. Add pepper strips and ¼ teaspoon freshly ground black pepper; continue to cook 3 minutes, tossing, or until peppers are slightly softened. Remove from heat; let cool.
2. Flatten and stretch or roll dough into 13-inch round and transfer to lightly oiled pizza pan. Spread sauce on dough to within 1 inch of edge. Scatter half the mozzarella over sauce, then top with sausage mixture; scatter remaining mozzarella on top. Sprinkle with Parmesan, if using.
3. Bake until cheese is melted and bubbly, and edges of pizza are well browned and crusty, about 10 minutes. Cut into 8 slices.

Each serving About 761 calories, 32 g protein, 64 g carbohydrate, 41 g total fat (16 g saturated), 2 g fiber, 99 mg cholesterol, 1,334 mg sodium.

Pizza Pronto

From Redbook

Total time **10 minutes**

MAKES 4 MAIN-DISH SERVINGS

- 4 pocketless pita breads (7-inch)
- 1 Tbsp. basil-flavored olive oil
- 2 Tbsp. tapenade (olive paste)
- 8 thin slices soppressata
- 4 oz. fresh mozzarella cheese, thinly sliced
- 1 red bell pepper, seeded and cut into strips
- 1 yellow bell pepper, seeded and cut into strips
- 16 slices plum tomato
- 1 cup grated fontina cheese
- ¼ cup freshly grated Parmesan cheese
- ½ cup arugula leaves

1. Adjust oven rack to bottom position. Preheat oven to 500°F.
2. Place pita breads on large baking sheet. Brush each with oil, then spread on tapenade, dividing evenly. Place soppressata, then mozzarella, on pitas. Scatter bell peppers, tomatoes, and fontina on top. Bake 5 to 7 minutes, until crust is crisp and cheese is melted. Remove from oven. Sprinkle with Parmesan; top with arugula.

Each serving About 612 calories, 29 g protein, 54 g carbohydrate, 31 g total fat (14 g saturated), 4 g fiber, 74 mg cholesterol, 1,415 mg sodium.

Mexican Pizza

From Good Housekeeping

Total time **15 minutes**

MAKES 4 MAIN-DISH SERVINGS

- ½ **cup prepared black bean dip**
- 1 **large (12-inch) thin ready-made pizza crust**
- ½ **cup shredded Mexican cheese blend**
- 1 **ripe avocado, cut into chunks**
- 2 **limes, zested and juiced**
- 2 **cups shredded romaine lettuce**
- 1 **medium tomato, chopped**

1. Preheat outdoor grill for direct grilling on medium.
2. Spread bean dip evenly on pizza crust, leaving ½-inch border; sprinkle with cheese. Place crust on hot grill; cover and grill until grill marks appear, 8 to 9 minutes. (Or, place crust on ungreased cookie sheet. Bake 8 to 10 minutes or until cheese melts.)
3. Meanwhile, in small bowl, gently stir avocado with 1 tablespoon lime juice. In another small bowl, toss romaine with ¼ teaspoon lime zest and 1 tablespoon juice.

4. Top pizza with romaine mixture and tomato, then with avocado.

Each serving About 310 calories, 13 g protein, 34 g carbohydrate, 15 g total fat (4 g saturated), 4 g fiber, 17 mg cholesterol, 520 mg sodium.

1 Tapenade on Toasts

Preheat oven to 475°F. In bowl, mix 2 teaspoons **olive oil** with 1 **garlic** clove, crushed. Brush mixture over **crust;** cut into 12 wedges. Bake on cookie sheet 10 minutes or until golden brown. In food processor, pulse 1 cup pitted **kalamata olives, 2 anchovy fillets,** 2 garlic cloves, 2 tablespoons olive oil, and 1¼ teaspoons freshly ground **black pepper** until very finely chopped. Spread on toasts. Serves 6.

2 Pizza Panzanella Salad

Cut **crust** into 1-inch squares; in skillet on medium, cook 10 minutes or until crisp, stirring; let cool. In bowl, combine 2 pints **cherry tomatoes,** halved; 1 cup fresh **mini mozzarella balls,** quartered; ¼ cup fresh **basil** leaves, thinly sliced; 2 tablespoons **white wine vinegar;** ¼ teaspoon **salt;** and ¼ teaspoon freshly ground **black pepper** with crust pieces. Serves 4.

4
Ideas for...
Pizza Crust

Savor our new takes on this supermarket staple. It makes a mean grilled cheese and is terrific in salad!
Use a ready-made 12-inch thin pizza crust for each recipe.

From Good Housekeeping

3 Cheesy Panini

Cut **crust** in quarters. Thinly slice 1 ball (8 oz.) **fresh mozzarella.** On 1 quarter, arrange 1 layer mozzarella. Top with 3 slices **salami;** 3 slices deli-sliced **ham;** 2 **pepperoncini** (Tuscan peppers), split (discard stems and seeds); and 1 layer mozzarella. Top with 1 piece crust. Repeat to make another panini. Preheat indoor grill pan. Add panini, and weigh down with heavy skillet. Cook 8 minutes or until cheese melts, turning once. Cut each panini in half. Serves 4.

4 Zucchini Flatbread

Preheat oven to 475°F. In colander, toss 2 small **zucchini,** shredded, with ½ teaspoon **salt.** Let stand 10 minutes. Squeeze out all liquid. In bowl, combine zucchini with 1 cup grated **Gruyère cheese;** ¼ teaspoon fresh **thyme** leaves, chopped; and ¼ teaspoon crushed **red pepper flakes.** Spread mixture on crust. Place on cookie sheet; bake 15 minutes or until golden brown. Serves 6.

Sloppy **Janes**

From Redbook

Total time **15 minutes**

MAKES 4 MAIN-DISH SERVINGS

- 1 **Tbsp. canola oil**
- 1 **cup chopped green onions**
- 1 **cup chopped yellow and orange bell peppers**
- 1 **Tbsp. garlic paste**
- 1 **lb. ground turkey**
- 1 **can (14.5 oz.) fire-roasted diced tomatoes**
- 2 **Tbsp. Worcestershire sauce**
- 1 **chipotle chile in adobo sauce, chopped**
  Salt
- 4 **pieces cornbread or 4 toaster corncakes, halved**
- 1 **Tbsp. red wine vinegar**
- ¼ **cup chopped fresh cilantro**

1. In large nonstick skillet on medium-high, heat oil. Add onions and peppers; cook, stirring constantly, 2 minutes. Add garlic paste and cook, stirring constantly, 1 minute.

2. Add turkey and cook, breaking it up with wooden spoon, stirring until no longer pink, 3 minutes. Add tomatoes and their juices, Worcestershire sauce, chipotle chile, and ½ teaspoon salt. Reduce heat to medium and cook, covered, 3 minutes.

3. Meanwhile, toast cornbread or corncakes.

4. Stir vinegar and cilantro into cooked turkey mixture.

5. Spoon half of Sloppy Jane mixture over 4 slices cornbread, dividing evenly. Repeat with remaining Sloppy Jane mixture and cornbread.

Each serving About 374 calories, 26 g protein, 33 g carbohydrate, 15 g total fat (3 g saturated), 3 g fiber, 69 mg cholesterol, 893 mg sodium.

Turkey Club
Quesadillas

From Redbook

Total time **10 minutes**

MAKES 4 MAIN-DISH SERVINGS

- 8 **flour tortillas (8-inch)**
- 4 **oz. smoked turkey, sliced**
- 1 **chipotle chile in adobo sauce, finely chopped**
- ½ **cup sour cream**
- 4 **plum tomatoes, sliced**
- 8 **slices cooked bacon**
- 2 **cups shredded pepper jack cheese**
- 1 **cup shredded romaine or iceberg lettuce**
- **Guacamole and salsa (optional)**

1. Place 4 tortillas on work surface. Top each tortilla with turkey, chipotle chile, sour cream, tomatoes, bacon, cheese, and lettuce, dividing evenly. Place second tortilla on top of each.
2. Preheat large nonstick griddle or 2 large nonstick skillets. Place 2 quesadillas on griddle or in skillets. Cook, pressing down occasionally, until tortillas are browned on 1 side, about 2 minutes. Carefully flip and cook second side 2 minutes, or until tortillas are browned and cheese is melted. Repeat with 2 remaining quesadillas. Let sit 2 minutes; cut each quesadilla into 4 wedges. Top with guacamole and salsa, if desired.

Each serving without toppings About 590 calories, 35 g protein, 38 g carbohydrate, 36 g total fat (17 g saturated), 5 g fiber, 93 mg cholesterol, 1,131 mg sodium.

LATIN-AMERICAN
When the classic turkey club meets the quesadilla, the result is a winner!

Fish **Tacos**

From Good Housekeeping

Total time **15 minutes**

MAKES 4 MAIN-DISH SERVINGS

- 4 **cups shredded cabbage mix for coleslaw (half 16 oz. bag)**
- 2 **limes, zested and juiced**
- ½ **cup reduced-fat sour cream**
- 1 **Tbsp. olive oil**
- 1¼ **lb. tilapia fillets**
- ¼ **tsp. ground chipotle chile pepper**
  Salt
- 8 **corn tortillas**
- 1 **cup salsa**

1. In large bowl, combine cabbage mix and ¼ cup lime juice; set aside. In small bowl, stir 2 teaspoons lime zest into sour cream; set aside.

2. In 12-inch skillet on medium-high, heat oil until hot. On sheet of waxed paper, sprinkle tilapia fillets with chipotle chile pepper and ¼ teaspoon salt to season both sides. Add fish to skillet, and cook 5 to 6 minutes or until it turns opaque throughout, turning once. Meanwhile, warm tortillas.

3. To serve, cut fillets into 8 pieces. Place 2 pieces tilapia in each tortilla; top tacos with slaw, lime sour cream, and salsa.

Each serving About 360 calories, 28 g protein, 37 g carbohydrate, 12 g total fat (3 g saturated), 4 g fiber, 12 mg cholesterol, 790 mg sodium.

Tex-Mex **Chicken** Tacos *with* Chili Onion Rings

From Redbook

Total time **15 minutes**

MAKES 4 MAIN-DISH SERVINGS

- 1¼ **lb. skinless, boneless chicken breast**
- ¼ **cup bottled garlic-lime marinade**
- ¾ **tsp. ancho chile powder**
  Salt and pepper
- 1 **can (11 oz.) Mexi-corn, rinsed and drained**
- ¼ **cup fire-roasted salsa verde**
- ¼ **cup diced red onion**
- 2 **Tbsp. chopped fresh cilantro**
- 1 **Tbsp. fresh lime juice**
- ½ **cup french-fried onion rings**
- 8 **corn taco shells**
- 1 **cup shredded romaine lettuce**

1. In medium bowl, toss chicken with marinade, ½ teaspoon chile powder, ½ teaspoon salt, and ¼ teaspoon freshly ground black pepper.

2. In another bowl, combine Mexi-corn, salsa, onion, cilantro, and lime juice.

3. Preheat outdoor grill or indoor grill pan to medium. Cook chicken 3 to 4 minutes per side until cooked through.

4. Meanwhile, in skillet on medium, toss onion rings with remaining ¼ teaspoon chile powder; heat onion rings 3 minutes, until warm, stirring.

5. Cut chicken into ½-inch pieces. Fill each taco shell with chicken, dividing evenly. Top each with 2 tablespoons corn mixture and 2 tablespoons onion-ring mixture. Garnish with lettuce.

Each serving About 387 calories, 33 g protein, 33 g carbohydrate, 13 g total fat (3 g saturated), 2 g fiber, 78 mg cholesterol, 1,208 mg sodium.

Black Bean & Corn **Tostadas**

From Redbook

Total time **10 minutes**

MAKES 4 MAIN-DISH SERVINGS

   Nonstick olive oil cooking spray
2 **cups fresh or frozen (thawed) corn kernels**
1 **large zucchini (diced)**
1½ **cups quartered grape tomatoes**
⅓ **cup chopped red onion**
¼ **cup chopped fresh cilantro**
1 **seeded and minced chipotle chile in adobo sauce plus 2 tsp. adobo sauce from can**
2 **Tbsp. fresh lime juice**
   Kosher salt
1 **cup vegetarian refried black beans**
8 **crisp tostada shells**
1 **cup shredded romaine lettuce**
1 **Hass avocado, sliced**
½ **cup crumbled queso fresco**

1. Spray large nonstick skillet with cooking spray; heat on medium-high. Add corn and zucchini, and cook 3 minutes; transfer to bowl. Stir in tomatoes, onion, cilantro, chipotle chile, adobo sauce, lime juice, and ½ teaspoon salt.

2. In microwave-safe bowl, reheat black beans.

3. Spread each tostada shell with 2 tablespoons beans and top with shredded lettuce. Spoon corn mixture over lettuce, then top with avocado slices and queso fresco.

Each serving About 362 calories, 13 g protein, 47 g carbohydrate, 17 g total fat (4 g saturated), 11 g fiber, 10 mg cholesterol, 482 mg sodium.

IT'S DONE!
These open-faced Mexican sandwiches are incredibly fast to make—and vegetarian.

Sammies aren't just for lunch—they're a great shortcut to an easy dinner that you can make (and eat) in record time

SUPER-SIMPLE
SANDWICHES

Reuben **Wraps**

From Redbook

Total time **10 minutes**

MAKES 4 WRAPS

- **2 cups coleslaw mix**
- **1 cup shredded carrots**
- **2 Tbsp. cider vinegar**
- **6 Tbsp. Thousand Island dressing**
- **4 whole wheat or multi-grain tortillas or wraps (8-inch)**
- **4 romaine or butter lettuce leaves**
- **8 thin slices turkey (about ½ lb.)**
- **8 thin slices Gruyère or other Swiss cheese**

1. In bowl, combine coleslaw mix, carrots, cider vinegar, and 2 tablespoons dressing.
2. Spread tortillas or wraps with remaining 4 tablespoons dressing. Layer each wrap with 1 lettuce leaf, 2 slices turkey, and 2 slices cheese. Top each with about ⅓ cup coleslaw. Roll up burrito-style, tucking in sides.

Each wrap About 528 calories, 32 g protein, 44 g carbohydrate, 29 g total fat (12 g saturated), 5 g fiber, 89 mg cholesterol, 1,196 mg sodium.

STANDOUT WRAPS

Crunchy coleslaw and creamy Thousand Island dressing make these sandwiches special.

Chicken Caesar
Pitas

From Good Housekeeping
Active time **10 minutes**
Total time **15 minutes**

MAKES 4 MAIN-DISH SERVINGS

- 3 Tbsp. extra virgin olive oil, plus additional for greasing pan
- ¾ lb. chicken-breast tenders
  Salt and pepper
- 2 Tbsp. fresh lemon juice
- 1 Tbsp. red wine vinegar
- 1 tsp. Dijon mustard
- 1 tsp. anchovy paste (optional)
- 1 garlic clove, cut in half
- 4 whole wheat pitas (6½-inch), each cut in half
- 1 romaine lettuce heart, chopped
- ¼ cup fresh basil leaves, sliced
- ¼ cup shredded Parmesan cheese
- 1 cup grape tomatoes, each cut in half

1. Preheat indoor grill pan on medium-high. Lightly brush with oil. Sprinkle chicken with ⅛ teaspoon salt and ⅛ teaspoon freshly ground black pepper. Cook 6 to 7 minutes or until chicken is browned and just loses its pink color throughout, turning once. Transfer chicken to cutting board and let cool completely.
2. Meanwhile, in large bowl, with wire whisk, stir lemon juice, vinegar, mustard, ⅛ teaspoon salt, ⅛ teaspoon pepper, and anchovy paste, if using, until well mixed. While whisking, add oil in steady stream until incorporated.
3. Rub cut sides of garlic clove all over insides of pitas; discard garlic. Microwave pitas on High 15 seconds.
4. Cut chicken into 1-inch pieces. In bowl with dressing, combine lettuce, basil, Parmesan, tomatoes, and cooked chicken, tossing to coat. Stuff salad mixture into pita halves.

Each serving About 340 calories, 25 g protein, 29 g carbohydrate, 15 g total fat (3 g saturated), 4 g fiber, 52 mg cholesterol, 540 mg sodium.

Chipotle-spiced meat and tangy blue cheese add up to a mouthful of great taste.

Spicy **BBQ Burgers** *with* Blue Cheese Slaw

From Redbook

Total time **15 minutes**

MAKES 4 BURGERS

- **2 cups shredded carrots**
- **⅓ cup bottled or homemade blue-cheese dressing**
- **1 Tbsp. fresh lemon juice**
- **1½ lb. ground beef**
- **½ cup smoky chipotle chile barbecue sauce (or favorite barbecue sauce mixed with 1 minced chipotle chile in adobo sauce)**
- **½ tsp. ground chipotle chile pepper**
- **½ tsp. ground cumin**
-   **Salt**
- **4 hamburger buns, split**
- **1 Tbsp. canola oil**
- **4 romaine lettuce leaves**

1. In medium bowl, combine carrots, dressing, and lemon juice.

2. Preheat outdoor grill or indoor grill pan on medium. In medium bowl, gently mix beef, ¼ cup barbecue sauce (or barbecue sauce mixture), chipotle, cumin, and 1 teaspoon salt. Divide mixture evenly and shape into 4 patties, each about ¾-inch thick.

3. Brush hamburger buns with oil, then toast on grill, 1 to 2 minutes; set aside. Grill burgers 3 to 4 minutes per side for medium-rare, brushing with remaining ¼ cup barbecue sauce (or barbecue sauce mixture).

4. On each bun bottom, place lettuce leaf, then burger, then slaw. Replace top half of bun.

Each burger About 597 calories, 36 g protein, 40 g carbohydrate, 32 g total fat (9 g saturated), 3 g fiber, 107 mg cholesterol, 1,307 mg sodium.

BBQ Pork Burgers

From Redbook

Total time **15 minutes**

MAKES 4 BURGERS

- ½ **lb. ground pork**
- ½ **cup barbecue sauce**
- 1 **Tbsp. Dijon mustard**
  Salt and pepper
- 2 **oz. sliced Monterey Jack or Muenster cheese**
- 4 **hamburger buns, split and grilled or toasted**
- 1⅓ **cups coleslaw**
  Potato chips and pickles (optional)

1. In medium bowl, gently mix pork, ¼ cup barbecue sauce, mustard, ½ teaspoon salt, and ¼ teaspoon freshly ground black pepper. Divide mixture evenly into 4 patties.
2. Preheat outdoor grill or indoor grill pan on medium-high. Place burgers on hot grill. Cook burgers 5 minutes per side, until browned and cooked through, brushing them with remaining ¼ cup barbecue sauce. Place cheese on burgers during last 1 to 2 minutes of cooking time, with grill covered, to melt cheese.
3. Place each burger on bottom of each hamburger bun; top with coleslaw, dividing evenly. Serve with potato chips and pickles, if desired.

Each burger without chips and pickles About 451 calories, 19 g protein, 42 g carbohydrate, 22 g total fat (8 g saturated), 2 g fiber, 57 mg cholesterol, 1,096 mg sodium.

PAIR THEM UP

The creamy mildness of ripe avocado wedges is the perfect complement to the spices in these burgers.

5 INGREDIENTS

Chipotle Nacho
Burgers

From Good Housekeeping

Total time **15 minutes**

MAKES 4 BURGERS

- 1¼ **lb. lean ground beef (90%)**
- 1½ **tsp. ground chipotle chile pepper**
       Salt
       Nonstick cooking spray
- 4   **slices (1 oz. each) pepper Jack or Monterey Jack cheese**
- 4   **hamburger buns, split and toasted**
- 1   **cup mild or medium salsa**

1. In large bowl, with hand, mix beef, chipotle, and ¼ teaspoon salt until blended, but do not overmix. Shape beef mixture into four 3½-inch patties, handling meat as little as possible for best texture.
2. Lightly spray indoor grill pan or 12-inch skillet with nonstick cooking spray, then heat on medium until hot.
3. Place burgers in hot pan. For medium, cook 6 minutes, turn burgers over, and cook 3 minutes longer. Top each

burger with 1 slice cheese; cook 2 to 3 minutes or until cheese melts.
4. To serve, place burgers on buns and top with salsa.

Each burger About 495 calories, 40 g protein, 26 g carbohydrate, 24 g total fat (11 g saturated), 4 g fiber, 121 mg cholesterol, 830 mg sodium.

Philly **Cheesesteak** Sandwiches

From Redbook
Total time **12 minutes**
MAKES 4 SANDWICHES

- **4** pieces focaccia (about 5 inches long), or 4 ciabatta rolls, halved
- **5** Tbsp. garlic- or basil-flavored olive oil
- **3** red, yellow, and/or green bell peppers, cut into strips
- **1** red onion, sliced
- **2** Tbsp. chopped oil-packed sun-dried tomatoes
- **10** oz. skirt steak, cut into thin strips, or pepper beef strips
  Salt and pepper
- **8** thin slices provolone cheese (about 4 oz.)

1. Brush cut halves of bread with 1 tablespoon oil. In large nonstick skillet on medium, toast bread, cut sides down, until lightly browned. Remove from pan; set aside.
2. In same skillet on medium-high, heat remaining 4 tablespoons oil. Add peppers, onion, and tomatoes, and cook 3 to 4 minutes, until vegetables are crisp-tender. Add steak, sprinkle with ¼ teaspoon salt and ¼ teaspoon freshly ground black pepper, and cook 2 to 3 minutes longer.
3. Place steak mixture on each bottom piece of bread, dividing evenly. Top each with 2 slices provolone. Place top of bread on cheese; serve immediately.

Each sandwich About 600 calories, 29 g protein, 49 g carbohydrate, 33 g total fat (10 g saturated), 4 g fiber, 66 mg cholesterol, 851 mg sodium.

Cheesy Meatball Heroes

From Redbook

Total time **15 minutes**

MAKES 4 SANDWICHES

- **16** frozen meatballs or fresh, fully cooked meatballs
- **1** jar (15.5 oz.) marinara sauce
- **½** cup sun-dried tomato pesto
- **4** hero or ciabatta rolls, cut in half and toasted
- **4** Tbsp. freshly grated Parmesan cheese
- **4** oz. sliced or shredded provolone cheese
- **4** oz. sliced or shredded fontina cheese

1. Preheat oven to 400°F. If using frozen meatballs, cook according to directions.
2. Meanwhile, in medium saucepan on medium, heat marinara sauce and meatballs, stirring frequently, until sauce is thickened and hot, 5 to 6 minutes.
3. Spread 1 tablespoon pesto sauce on bottom of each roll. Place 4 meatballs on each roll. Spoon sauce on top of meatballs. Sprinkle each hero with 1 tablespoon Parmesan. Top each with 1 ounce provolone and 1 ounce fontina. Place heroes on baking sheet; bake 4 to 5 minutes or until cheeses are melted. Serve with tossed salad, if you like.

Each sandwich About 842 calories, 40 g protein, 61 g carbohydrate, 49 g total fat (20 g saturated), 7 g fiber, 107 mg cholesterol, 2,052 mg sodium.

MIXED BITTER GREENS

From Good Housekeeping

Total time **15 minutes**

MAKES 12 SIDE-DISH SERVINGS

In small bowl, whisk together ¼ cup **balsamic vinegar,** 2 tablespoons pure **honey,** 1 tablespoon **Dijon mustard,** ¼ teaspoon **salt,** and ½ teaspoon freshly ground **black pepper.** Slowly whisk in ½ cup **extra virgin olive oil** until well blended; set aside dressing.

In large bowl, combine 1 head **escarole,** chopped; 2 small heads **radicchio,** sliced; 5 ounces **arugula** leaves; ½ cup slivered **almonds,** toasted; and dressing. Toss until greens are evenly coated. With vegetable peeler, shave 3 ounces **Parmesan cheese** over salad.

Each serving About 170 calories, 5 g protein, 7 g carbohydrate, 14 g total fat (3 g saturated), 2 g fiber, 6 mg cholesterol, 200 mg sodium.

Lobster **BLT CLub**

From Redbook
Total time **15 minutes**
MAKES 4 SANDWICHES

- ¾ **cup light mayonnaise**
- 1 **lime, zested and juiced**
- 1 **lemon, zested and juiced**
  Kosher salt and pepper
- 8 **slices smoked bacon**
- 12 **slices (½-inch-thick) brioche
  or challah bread**
- 1 **lb. cooked lobster meat, cut
  into bite-size pieces**
- 8 **small Boston lettuce leaves**
- 8 **thin slices tomato**

1. In small bowl, combine mayonnaise, ¼ teaspoon lime zest, ¼ teaspoon lemon zest, 1½ teaspoons lime juice, 1½ teaspoons lemon juice, ¼ teaspoon salt, and ¼ teaspoon freshly ground black pepper until blended. Set aside citrus mayo.

2. In large nonstick skillet on medium, cook bacon until crisp, about 8 minutes, turning once. Drain on paper towels.

3. Meanwhile, preheat broiler. Place bread on baking sheet and place under broiler until first side is lightly toasted, turning sheet pan as bread toasts. Turn slices over to toast other sides.

4. In medium bowl, combine lobster, 3 tablespoons citrus mayo, and ¼ teaspoon salt. Spread citrus mayo on 1 side of bread slices.

5. Place lettuce leaves on mayonnaise side of 4 bread slices. Top with lobster. Place a second bread slice, mayonnaise side up, on top of lobster, pressing down. Top with remaining lettuce leaves, 2 tomato slices, 2 strips bacon (folded to fit), and remaining 4 bread slices, mayonnaise side down. Press sandwiches together. Place toothpicks into each sandwich; cut sandwiches diagonally into quarters.

Each sandwich About 600 calories, 37 g protein, 49 g carbohydrate, 28 g total fat (6 g saturated), 3 g fiber, 245 mg cholesterol, 1,893 mg sodium.

DELICIOUS
INDULGENCE
When the classic
lobster roll meets the BLT,
who can resist?

Buffalo Shrimp
Sliders

From Redbook

Total time **10 minutes**

MAKES 4 MAIN-DISH SERVINGS

- 8 **soft dinner rolls (3-inch), split**
- 1 **small heart romaine lettuce, finely shredded (2 cups)**
- 1 **celery stalk, halved lengthwise and thinly sliced**
- ⅓ **cup shredded carrots**
- 3 **Tbsp. bottled or homemade blue-cheese dressing**
  Nonstick cooking spray
- 2 **Tbsp. unsalted butter, softened**
- 1 **lb. medium shrimp, peeled and deveined**
- 3 **Tbsp. hot pepper sauce or Buffalo-wing sauce**
- ¼ **cup crumbled blue cheese**

1. Preheat broiler. Place dinner rolls, cut side up, on baking sheet. Place under broiler and lightly toast, turning baking sheet to toast rolls evenly.
2. In medium bowl, combine lettuce, celery, carrots, and dressing. Divide mixture over bottom halves of rolls.
3. Coat large nonstick skillet with nonstick cooking spray and heat on medium-high. Add 1 tablespoon butter and shrimp; cook 2 minutes or until shrimp are almost cooked through.
4. Add remaining 1 tablespoon butter and hot sauce to skillet; continue to cook, stirring shrimp in sauce with spoon, until cooked through, about 1 minute. Spoon shrimp and sauce over lettuce mixture, sprinkle with blue-cheese crumbles, and replace tops of rolls, toasted side down.

Each serving About 420 calories, 28 g protein, 34 g carbohydrate, 20 g total fat (8 g saturated), 2 g fiber, 168 mg cholesterol, 1064 mg sodium.

Crispy Fish
Sandwiches

From Good Housekeeping
Active time **10 minutes**
Total time **15 minutes**

MAKES 4 SANDWICHES

Nonstick cooking spray

3 **cups shredded red cabbage (6 oz.)**

2 **Tbsp. apple cider vinegar**

½ **tsp. celery seeds**

¼ **cup fresh flat-leaf parsley leaves, finely chopped**

¼ **cup plain fat-free Greek yogurt**

2 **Tbsp. light mayonnaise**

2 **Tbsp. sweet pickle relish**

1 **Tbsp. fresh lemon juice**

1 **tsp. Dijon mustard**

Salt and pepper

2 **large egg whites**

¾ **cup plain dried bread crumbs**

4 **skinless flounder fillets (4 oz. each)**

4 **whole wheat hamburger buns, toasted**

½ **seedless (English) cucumber, very thinly sliced**

1. Arrange oven rack 4 inches from heat source. Preheat broiler on high. Lightly coat 18″ by 12″ jelly-roll pan with nonstick cooking spray.
2. In large bowl, combine cabbage, vinegar, and celery seeds; toss well. Set slaw aside.
3. In small bowl, with whisk, combine parsley, yogurt, mayonnaise, relish, lemon juice, mustard, ¼ teaspoon salt, and ⅛ teaspoon freshly ground black pepper; cover tartar sauce and refrigerate.

4. In pie plate, whisk egg whites with fork just until frothy. Place bread crumbs on waxed paper. Sprinkle flounder fillets with ¼ teaspoon salt and ¼ teaspoon pepper to season both sides. Dip fillets into egg whites, then coat with bread crumbs, patting on crumbs to cover both sides. Arrange fillets on prepared pan. Broil fish 2½ to 3 minutes or until fillets are golden brown on both sides, turning over once.

5. Cut each fillet in half. On bottom of each bun, spread 2 tablespoons tartar sauce; top with cucumber, 2 pieces flounder, and ¾ cup slaw. Replace tops of buns to serve.

Each sandwich About 365 calories, 30 g protein, 46 g carbohydrate, 7 g total fat (1 g saturated), 6 g fiber, 56 mg cholesterol, 930 mg sodium.

Add a few easy extras and transform fast food into a healthy feast! How simple (and how yummy) is that?

TAKEOUT
MAGIC

Sesame-**Noodle** Toss

From Good Housekeeping

Total time **10 minutes**

MAKES 4 MAIN-DISH SERVINGS

- **1** large takeout order Chinese cold sesame noodles
- **3** Tbsp. seasoned rice vinegar
- **6** oz. deli-sliced, no-salt-added turkey breast, cut into strips
- **¼** head iceberg lettuce, sliced
- **1** cup packaged shredded carrots
- **½** seedless cucumber, unpeeled and thinly sliced
- Cayenne pepper sauce

In large bowl, toss sesame noodles with vinegar and 1 tablespoon water until well mixed. Add turkey, lettuce, carrots, and cucumber. Toss until combined. (Add additional water by tablespoon if salad seems dry.) Serve with cayenne pepper sauce.

Each serving About 565 calories, 24 g protein, 60 g carbohydrate, 27 g total fat (4 g saturated), 5 g fiber, 19 mg cholesterol, 1,410 mg sodium.

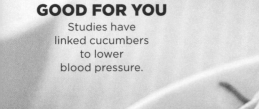

GOOD FOR YOU
Studies have
linked cucumbers
to lower
blood pressure.

DID YOU KNOW?

Edamame lowers cholesterol.

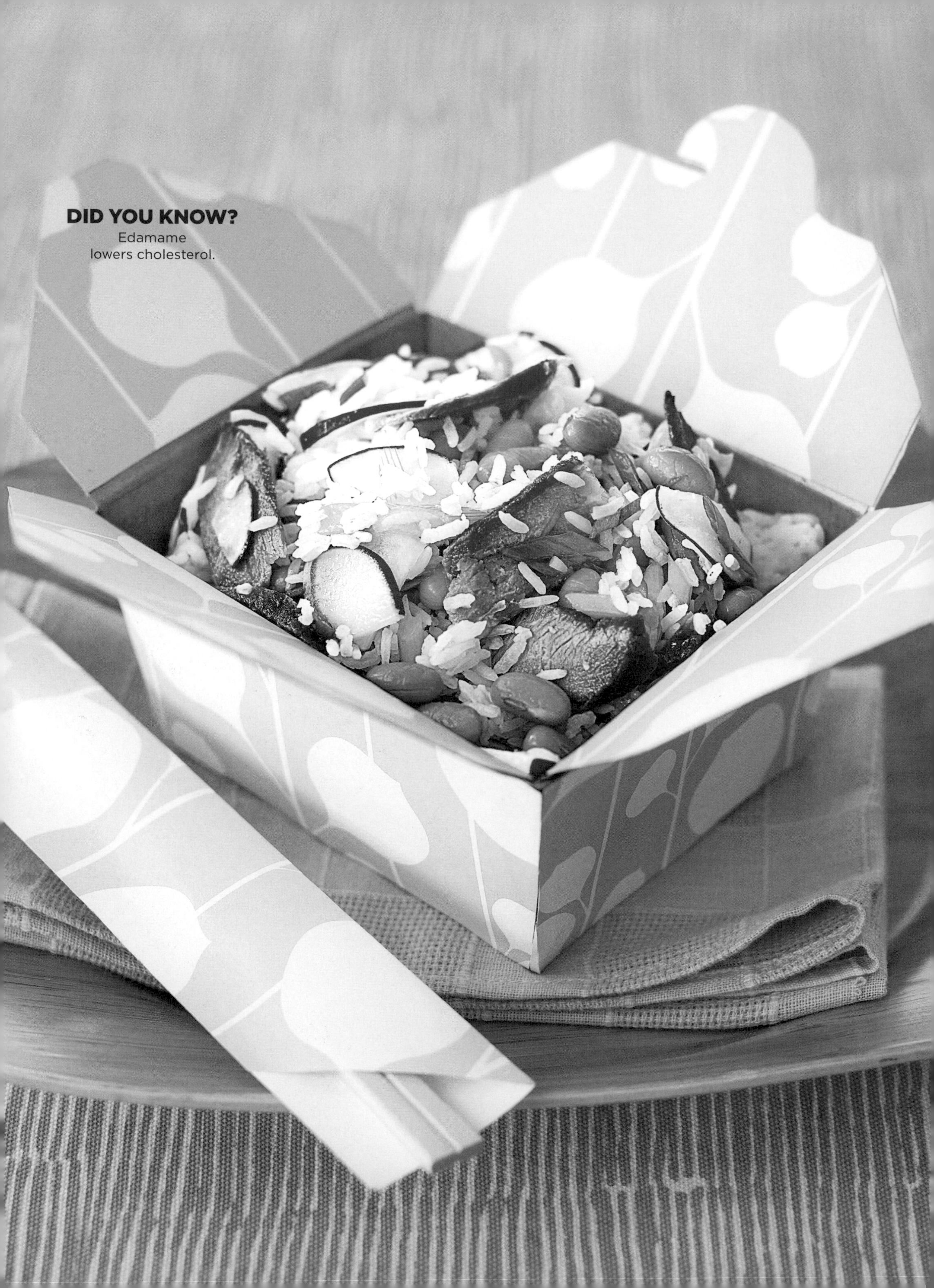

4 INGREDIENTS

Asian **Rice** Salad

From Good Housekeeping

Total time **7 minutes**

MAKES 4 MAIN-DISH SERVINGS

- ½ **cup frozen shelled edamame or peas**
- 1 **large takeout order Chinese roast pork, cut in strips**
- 1 **small takeout order Chinese white rice**
- 2 **green onions, thinly sliced**
- 4 **large radishes, thinly sliced**
- 2 **Tbsp. seasoned rice vinegar**
- 1 **Tbsp. Asian sesame oil**

1. In colander, rinse edamame under hot water to thaw; drain well.
2. In medium bowl, toss pork, rice, onions, radishes, edamame, vinegar, and oil until combined.

Each serving About 520 calories, 26 g protein, 46 g carbohydrate, 25 g total fat (7 g saturated), 2 g fiber, 71 mg cholesterol, 980 mg sodium.

EXTRA RICE IS NICE

A leftover carton of white, or better yet, brown, rice is a first-class meal multiplier—just mix it with a few fresh ingredients. Try:

- Stirring it into chicken broth with baby spinach for soup; top with grated Parmesan.
- Sautéeing it with green onions and peas.
- Adding it to prepared vanilla pudding for rice pudding.
- Heating it, then topping with maple syrup, nuts, or honey for a morning meal.

Stir-fry in Lettuce Cups

From Good Housekeeping

Total time **6 minutes**

MAKES 4 MAIN-DISH SERVINGS

- 2½ **cups broccoli slaw (half 12 oz. package)**
- 1 **large head Boston lettuce**
- 1 **small takeout order Chinese white rice**
- 1 **large takeout order Chinese chicken and peanut stir-fry**

1. Place broccoli slaw in microwave-safe bowl. Cover and microwave on High 1 minute or until slightly softened.
2. Meanwhile, rinse and drain lettuce; separate head into 16 leaves.
3. To assemble, on each lettuce leaf, put 1 tablespoon rice, 1 tablespoon slaw, and ¼ cup stir-fry. Fold leaves over to eat.

Each serving About 630 calories, 38 g protein, 55 g carbohydrate, 29 g total fat (5 g saturated), 7 g fiber, 95 mg cholesterol, 1,265 mg sodium.

4 INGREDIENTS

Chili-Stuffed **Tomatoes**

From Good Housekeeping

Total time **15 minutes**

MAKES 4 MAIN-DISH SERVINGS

- 2 **large takeout orders chili**
- 1 **cup fresh or frozen (thawed) corn kernels**
- 4 **large tomatoes (12 to 14 oz. each)**

  Optional toppings: shredded iceberg or romaine lettuce, shredded Cheddar cheese, guacamole, chopped fresh cilantro leaves

1. In 2-quart saucepan, combine chili and corn. Cook on medium-low 10 minutes or until hot, stirring.
2. While chili heats, cut a slice from top of each tomato and reserve. With melon baller or spoon, hollow out tomatoes, leaving about ½-inch shell. (Reserve pulp for another use, or add some to chili if you like.) On microwave-safe plate lined with paper towels, place tomatoes, hollowed-sides down. Microwave on High 3 minutes or until tomatoes are warm.
3. Fill tomatoes with chili; serve with reserved tomato slices and your choice of toppings.

Each serving without toppings About 275 calories, 17 g protein, 42 g carbohydrate, 6 g total fat (2 g saturated), 9 g fiber, 28 mg cholesterol, 715 mg sodium.

No-Bake **Tamale** Pie

From Good Housekeeping

Total time **10 minutes**

MAKES 4 MAIN-DISH SERVINGS

- 2 **tsp. olive oil**
- 1 **log prepared polenta (12 oz.), cut into 12 rounds**
- 2 **large takeout orders chili**
- 1 **can (4 oz.) chopped mild green chiles**
- ½ **cup fresh cilantro leaves, chopped**

1. In nonstick 12-inch skillet on medium-high, heat oil. Add polenta rounds and cook about 2 minutes per side or until golden.
2. Meanwhile, in microwave-safe medium bowl, stir together takeout chili and chopped chiles with their liquid. Cover and microwave on High 1 to 2 minutes or until heated through. Stir in 3 tablespoons cilantro.
3. Spoon chili into shallow bowls. Top with polenta rounds and sprinkle with remaining cilantro.

Each serving About 250 calories, 14 g protein, 32 g carbohydrate, 7 g total fat (2 g saturated), 6 g fiber, 28 mg cholesterol, 960 mg sodium.

SURPRISING TIP

Corn is a great source of dietary fiber.

3 INGREDIENTS

White Pizza
with Fresh Tomato Topping

From Good Housekeeping

Total time **10 minutes**

MAKES 8 SLICES

- 1½ **lb. yellow and red tomatoes, cut into ½-inch chunks**
- ½ **cup fresh basil leaves, chopped**
- 1 **Tbsp. extra virgin olive oil**
- 1 **small garlic clove, crushed**
- ⅛ **tsp. crushed red pepper flakes**
  Salt
- 1 **large takeout white pizza**

In bowl, combine tomatoes, basil, oil, garlic, red pepper flakes, and ¼ teaspoon salt; toss. Spoon over hot pizza.

Each slice About 600 calories, 30 g protein, 63 g carbohydrate, 25 g total fat (10 g saturated), 3 g fiber, 55 mg cholesterol, 1,230 mg sodium.

4 INGREDIENTS

 +

Tuna Panzanella

From Good Housekeeping

Total time **15 minutes**

MAKES 4 MAIN-DISH SERVINGS

- **1 pint cherry tomatoes, each cut in half**
- **½ seedless cucumber, cut lengthwise into quarters, then thickly sliced**
- **¼ cup bottled red-wine vinaigrette or Italian dressing**
- **8 oz. takeout garlic knots or garlic breadsticks, cut into ¾-inch cubes**
- **1 can (6 oz.) white tuna in water, drained**
- **½ cup shaved Parmesan cheese**
- **½ cup fresh basil leaves, torn**
- **Romaine lettuce leaves**
- **Lemon wedges**

1. In large bowl, combine tomatoes, cucumber, and salad dressing. Add bread cubes, and toss to combine.
2. With fork, flake tuna into chunks. Add tuna, Parmesan, and basil to bowl; gently toss to combine. Serve salad with romaine and lemon wedges.

Each serving About 315 calories, 17 g protein, 33 g carbohydrate, 13 g total fat (4 g saturated), 2 g fiber, 21 mg cholesterol, 830 mg sodium.

3 INGREDIENTS

Hearty **Antipasto** Salad

From Good Housekeeping

Total time **10 minutes**

MAKES 4 MAIN-DISH SERVINGS

- **1 can (15 to 19 oz.) white kidney (cannellini) beans**
- **1 large takeout order antipasto salad (usually includes roasted peppers, prosciutto, artichokes, mozzarella, and grilled zucchini)**
- **1 package (5 oz.) baby arugula**
- **Olive oil and red wine vinegar (optional)**

Drain and rinse beans; put in large bowl. Cut ingredients from antipasto salad into bite-size pieces (you should get about 3 cups). Add to bowl, along with arugula. Toss together and serve with oil and vinegar, if desired.

Each serving without oil and vinegar About 230 calories, 13 g protein, 26 g carbohydrate, 8 g total fat (3 g saturated), 7 g fiber, 21 mg cholesterol, 785 mg sodium.

+  +

Buffalo **Chicken** Salad

5 INGREDIENTS

From Good Housekeeping

Total time **10 minutes**

MAKES 6 MAIN-DISH SERVINGS

- **2 bags (10 oz. each) romaine salad mix**
- **1 container (8 oz.) carrot and celery sticks, cut in ½-inch chunks**
- **1 takeout order chicken fingers or chicken nuggets (10 to 12 pieces), cut up**
- **2 Tbsp. cayenne pepper sauce**
- **½ cup bottled or homemade blue-cheese dressing**

Place romaine salad mix in large bowl. Top with carrot and celery pieces and cut-up chicken. Drizzle with pepper sauce. Serve with dressing.

Each serving About 355 calories, 16 g protein, 15 g carbohydrate, 22 g total fat (4 g saturated), 3 g fiber, 34 mg cholesterol, 1,090 mg sodium.

Shrimp Po'boys

From Good Housekeeping

Total time **10 minutes**

MAKES 4 SANDWICHES

- ⅓ **cup light mayonnaise**
- ½ **tsp. Cajun seasoning**
- 4 **hero rolls (6 inch each)**
- ½ **small head iceberg lettuce, thinly sliced**
- 2 **medium tomatoes, sliced**
- 2 **large takeout orders popcorn shrimp (about 1 lb.)**
- 1 **cup sliced dill pickles (optional)**

1. In small bowl, combine mayonnaise and Cajun seasoning. Cut each roll horizontally almost in half, leaving attached at 1 end. Scoop out about ½ inch soft bread from center of bottom halves.

2. Place rolls on serving plate. Spread mayo mixture on cut sides of top halves. Arrange lettuce, tomatoes, shrimp, and pickles, if using, on bottom halves.

Each sandwich About 465 calories, 16 g protein, 38 g carbohydrate, 28 g total fat (10 g saturated), 4 g fiber, 118 mg cholesterol, 1,470 mg sodium

Cocktail Sauce

- To make a speedy cup of salsa with a kick: Add 2 packets to chopped tomatoes and cilantro.
- Mix 1 packet into a tall glass of tomato juice with a splash of vodka for a quick Bloody Mary.

Tartar Sauce

- Combine 2 containers with chopped cucumber and 1 tablespoon chopped dill, and spread on grilled chicken or fish.
- Brush on 1 container per salmon fillet and broil for a yummy glaze.

Duck Sauce

- To create a flavorful condiment that tastes great on rotisserie chicken or grilled meats, combine with an equal amount of leftover hot Chinese mustard and add a dash of curry powder.

DON'T TOSS THE SAUCE

Are you always saving (but never using) the extra condiments that come with your takeout? Try these fast and tasty ways to put them to work.

- Combine 2 packets with 1 tablespoon light mayo and chopped green onion; spread on a tortilla, then top with smoked turkey. Call it a wrap.

Hot Sauce

- Stir 1 to 2 packets into a container of hummus, then use the mix as a dip with crudites or as a spread on a tomato sandwich.
- Drizzle over avocado slices for a delicious easier-than-guacamole Mexican side dish.

- Fake some lower-fat "buffalo wings" by tossing boneless chicken tenders in several packets before grilling them.

BBQ Sauce

- To add creamy tang to a burger or grilled chicken, top the meat with a mix of equal parts barbecue sauce and light mayo.
- In a blender, combine 1 can black beans, 1 garlic clove, and 2 or 3 packets barbecue sauce, and purée. Voilà—a smoky black bean dip.

Soy Sauce

- Create a super-fast Asian dressing by stirring 2 packets into ½ teaspoon grated fresh ginger and toasted sesame oil to taste.
- Mix 1 packet into 4 tablespoons softened butter and you've got a savory corn-on-the-cob topping.

1 Toasted Pound Cake with Pears

From Country Living

Total time **10 minutes**

MAKES 6 SERVINGS

In skillet on medium, melt 1½ tablespoons **unsalted butter.** Add 6 slices **pound cake** (each ¾-inch-thick), and toast until golden brown on both sides. Remove and keep warm. Slice 3 large, firm **Bosc pears** into ¾-inch thick slices. To same skillet, add pears and 3 tablespoons unsalted butter. Cook pears until golden brown on both sides, about 4 minutes. Serve pears with cake and store-bought **caramel sauce,** if desired.

Each serving without caramel sauce About 570 calories, 7 g protein, 71 g carbohydrate, 31 g total fat (14 g saturated), 4 g fiber, 270 mg cholesterol, 448 mg sodium.

4
Quick-Fix
Desserts

2 Grilled Peach Melba

From Good Housekeeping

Total time **10 minutes**

MAKES 6 SERVINGS

Preheat outdoor grill or indoor grill pan on medium until hot. Cut 3 large ripe **peaches** in half and discard pits. Place peach halves on hot grill, and cook 5 to 6 minutes or until lightly charred and tender, turning once. Meanwhile, in bowl, with fork, mash ½ pint fresh **raspberries** with 1½ tablespoons **sugar.** Stir in another ½ pint raspberries. To serve, place 1 peach half in each dessert bowl; top each with ½ cup **vanilla ice cream** and **raspberry sauce.**

Each serving About 218 calories, 4 g protein, 31 g carbohydrate, 9 g total fat (5 g saturated), 4 g fiber, 25 mg cholesterol, 35 mg sodium.

The perfect end to a weeknight meal? An insanely fast dessert!

3 Ice Cream Sandwiches

From Good Housekeeping

Total time **5 minutes**

MAKES 6 SERVINGS

Onto each of 6 thin, crispy **cookies,** scoop ½ cup slightly softened **ice cream** (any flavor; you'll need 3 cups total). Top each with another cookie; gently flatten.

Each serving About 200 calories, 4 g protein, 23 g carbohydrate, 11 g total fat (6 g saturated), 0 g fiber, 33 mg cholesterol, 58 mg sodium.

4 Chocolate-Hazelnut Panini

From Country Living

Total time **15 minutes**

MAKES 12 PANINI

Cut 1 loaf **ciabatta** into 4 (5″ by 3″) rectangles and split each horizontally. Cut 4 ounces **bittersweet chocolate** into 4 equal pieces. In small bowl, combine ½ cup **hazelnut butter** or almond butter, 2 tablespoons **honey,** ¼ teaspoon **salt,** and a dash of ground **cloves.** Spread 1 tablespoon mixture onto each bread bottom. Top each with 1 piece chocolate, and bread tops. In microwave, melt 2 tablespoons **unsalted butter.** Brush sandwiches with melted butter, and grill in panini press until chocolate melts. Cut each sandwich into 3 triangles and sprinkle with **sea salt.**

Each panini About 247 calories, 6 g protein, 30 g carbohydrate, 13 g total fat (4 g saturated), 3 g fiber, 5 mg cholesterol, 292 mg sodium.

RECICPE INDEX

PHOTOGRAPHY CREDITS

Antonis Achilleos: 114 (2). Jesus Ayala/
Studio D: 8, 14, 112. Quentin Bacon: 78. Iain
Bagwell: 90, 93, 95. James Baigrie: 26, 89,
98, 99, 105, 106, 107, 109, 111 (2), 114. James
Baigrie/Getty Images: 50. Mary Ellen
Bartley/Getty Images: 111. Matt Bowman/
Getty Images: 110. C Squared Studios/
Getty Images: 8. Steve Cohen/Getty
Images: 108, 109. Gemma Comas: 6 (2), 42,
51, 70, 80. Christopher Coppola/Studio D:
9. Davies and Starr/Getty Images: 51, 67,
112. Lilli Day/Getty Images: 62. Digital
Vision/Getty Images: 69 (2). Roger Dixon/
Getty Images: 44, 45, 50. Tara Donne: 1,
25, 81, 90, 108, 110, 112, 113, 115. Dorling
Kindersley/Getty Images: 3, 19, 26. Chris
Eckert/Studio D: 42, 50. Ylva Erevall/
Studio D: 50. Foodcollection/Getty
Images: 12, 21, 26, 40, 43, 52, 68. Jim
Franco: 2, 54, 101, 102. Philip Friedman/
Studio D: 3, 5 (2), 7 (2), 12, 14, 16, 18 (3), 19,
20, 21 (2), 25 (3), 26 (2), 27 (2), 37, 39 (2),
42 (3), 52 (2), 53, 61, 62 (3), 63 (2), 67, 69,
70 (2), 71, 75, 80, 84, 97 (3), 107, 111, 112.
Hayley Harrison: 41. Image Source/Getty
Images: 20, 63, 107. istockphoto: 21.
Frances Janisch: 22, 34, 53, 76. Jonathan
Kantor/Getty Images: 8. Dave King/Getty
Images: 8. Joerg Lehmann/Getty Images:
87. Charlotte Jenks Lewis/Studio D: 69, 70,
71. Kate Mathis: 24, 41, 73, 77, 94, 99, 103,
116. Andrew McCaul: iv bottom, 5, 14 (2), 16
(2), 18, 25 (2), 33, 37 (4), 56, 68, 69 (3), 74,
79, 84, 115. Marko Metzinger/Studio D: 5, 8,
40, 52, 67, 80 (2). Paul Moore/Getty
Images: 110. J Muckle/Studio D: 16, 42, 43,
44, 50, 51, 61, 66 (2), 67 (2), 68, 69 (2), 70,
75, 80, 97, 107, 111, 112. Thomas Albert
Eduard Müller/Getty Images: 51. Ngoc
Minh Ngo: 44. Kana Okada: 1, 21, 27, 40, 43,
44, 63, 68. Roger Phillips/Getty Images: 12,
19. Judd Pilossof/Getty Images: 114. Paul
Poplis/Getty Images: 87. Con Poulos: iv
top, 16, 35. Lara Robby/Studio D: 3, 5, 9, 20
(2), 21, 26, 27 (2), 32, 40, 51 (2), 75 (2), 80,
108 (2), 109 (2), 112 (2). Michael Rosenfeld/
Getty Images: 69, 75. James Ross/Getty
Images: 87. Tina Rupp: 17, 27, 28, 31, 36, 37,
49, 59, 60, 71 (3), 83, 84 (5), 88, 91. Charles
Schiller: 21. Kate Sears: 12, 20, 38, 50, 61,
62, 67, 69, 75, 86, 97. Ellen Silverman: 1 (2),
3 (2), 4, 13, 15, 19 (3), 32 (5), 45, 52, 56, 61
(3), 65, 66 (5), 70, 71, 85, 96, 115. Stock-
byte/Getty Images: 39, 43. Clive Streeter/
Getty Images: 53. David Turner/Studio D:
43, 62, 68, 69, 110 (2). Jonny Valiant: 11.
Visual Cuisines/Getty Images: 40. Russel
Wasserfall/Getty Images: 87. Michael
Weschler: 29. Jeff Westbrook/Studio D: 8.
Anna Williams: 46, 47 (4). Steve Wisbauer/
Getty Images: 9. Romulo Yanes: 57.

Front Cover: Jonny Valiant
Front Inside Flap: Andrew McCaul
Back Cover: Ellen Silverman (5); Lara
Robby/Studio D (potatoes)
Back Inside Flap: Tara Donne